THE COMMUNIST UNIVERSITY
OF LONDON

INTERNATIONAL BOOKSHOP PTY. LTD.
17 ELIZABETH STREET
MELBOURNE, AUSTRALIA, 3000
PHONE 61 2859

POLITICS, IDEOLOGY AND THE STATE

Papers from the Communist University of London

edited by SALLY HIBBIN

1978
LAWRENCE AND WISHART
LONDON

These papers were originally
delivered at the Communist University,
held in London in 1977.

Printed and bound in Great Britain at
The Camelot Press Ltd, Southampton

CONTENTS

PREFACE

In the ten years of its existence, the Communist University of London (CUL) has become one of the major national forums for the discussion and development of Marxist theory. One of its main strengths is its commitment to the tradition of Marxism as a creative and living theory, and it is to be hoped that this second collection of CUL papers reflects that strength.*

The sessions at the CUL are diverse and the speakers cover a wide range of topics from academic disciplines to current political questions. The CUL has been highly successful in creating an atmosphere in which many varied approaches to Marxism can be heard. No 'Marxist truth' is handed out in its sessions, but rather, through the interchange of theories and ideas, Marxism becomes alive and the CUL makes a contribution to its development. Many of the recent writings of the 'New Left' from Poulantzas to Colletti, from structuralism to feminism, have enriched this process.

CUL 9, held in 1977, was of course influenced by the discussion of the draft of the Communist Party's programme, *The British Road to Socialism*, and many of the sessions reflected this emphasis on strategy. The theory of the state, its nature in advanced capitalist societies, how the ruling-class maintains power, the nature of ideology and the role of politics, all became major areas of debate. The work of Antonio Gramsci was central to many of these discussions, as one of the major twentieth-century Marxists who examined these problems particularly in relation to Western Europe. The concentration of this collection on politics and ideology was therefore the natural choice for this volume arising from that particular emphasis at CUL 9.

One of the most important theoretical influences on the CUL and on Marxism in general is absent from this volume. Feminism has not only influenced our thinking about women, personal relationships and our style of work, it has also influenced Marxist thinking on strategy. The emergence of the Women's Movement and other social forces in the late

* The first collection, *Class, Hegemony and Party*, edited by Jon Bloomfield, appeared in 1977.

sixties undoubtedly sharpened the need for a more adequate political conception of alliances – one of the central ideas in *The British Road to Socialism*. Feminism also affected the CUL. For the first time a specialist course was organized on Sexual Politics. However, the course was organized along new lines; instead of the standard opening, discussion and reply, the women who led the sessions raised questions and problems that needed discussing within the overall context of the course. This led to a far greater participation in the course by everyone present, but corresponding difficulties in preparing a paper from the course for publication. We hope that in future collections this problem can be solved so that feminist theory can be properly represented in the written records of the CUL.

The impact of Marxist ideas, particularly in universities and colleges, is reflected not only by the continued growth of the CUL but also by the number of successful mini-CULs and Festivals of Marxism that take place around the country. To win the thousands of young people to Marxist ideas that are necessary to the fight for socialism in Britain, Marxism needs to be continually enriched by the experience and theory of all sections of society. The CUL, and this volume of papers, is a contribution to that development.

Editorial Committee on behalf of CUL
SALLY HIBBIN (ed.)
JOHN FAIRLEY
BETTY MATTHEWS
KEN SPOURS

ANNE SHOWSTACK SASSOON

HEGEMONY AND POLITICAL INTERVENTION

In the political debate on the left, and in a variety of academic
disciplines, there have been increasing references to Gramsci's concept
of hegemony usually assuming an understanding of the term without
discussing it theoretically. In current debates within Marxism,
particularly with regard to the attempt to develop a Marxist theory of
politics and the state, a hitherto relatively neglected area, Gramsci's
ideas have provided a focus of attention. In France and Italy they have
become the necessary elements for a wide-ranging discussion,
especially on the role of the revolutionary party, the question of
democracy and socialism, and the nature of a revolutionary strategy in
Western Europe.[1]* Most recently the possibility of analysing the
difficulties in building socialism in the USSR by using analytical tools
provided by Gramsci has been the starting point in a number of works.[2]
Moreover, criticisms of common elements in the strategy of a number of
communist parties, described as 'Eurocommunist', have been made by
criticizing Gramsci's concept of the state which, it is assumed, underlies
this strategy.[3]

At the same time, there has been a very incomplete discussion outside
France and Italy of the meaning and implications of hegemony. It must
be recognized immediately that this is an extremely difficult task. Any
study of Gramsci's thought encounters some very particular problems.
First of all, the nature of his texts is problematic. His pre-prison writings
are embedded in a situation characterized by the dramatic changes of
the years 1914–26. Written 'in haste', not intended to 'out-live' their
immediate purpose, these texts have the form of political journalism and
party documents.[4]

Secondly, the *Prison Notebooks* were written under difficult physical,
and intellectual conditions.[5] No longer writing as a political actor but re-
examining past experiences and the contemporary world as best he
could, Gramsci produced a series of notes which he considered

* See end of each essay for Notes.

unfinished fragments, elements and indications for further study.[6] His very language presents problems because he often used the same terms in different ways, and as the years passed, he increasingly used a code for possibly politically sensitive references.[7]

Difficulties in reading Gramsci also arise for a number of other reasons. There is, for example, a special problem in establishing the historical *context* of his thought, a problem which is related to the theoretical question of the object of his work. Until recently Gramsci was placed almost completely within the context of post-First World War Italy and the experiences of the Italian working-class movement in those years. Even this historical background has been examined in an uneven way. For example, his debate with Bordiga has mostly been investigated from a historical point of view rather than as providing an important element in the development of Gramsci's political thought.[8] Little is known about what is generally recognized as a crucial influence in Gramsci's political life, the period spent working for the Comintern in 1923–4 in Moscow and Vienna, and no thorough study of his writings between 1921 and 1926 has been published.[9] Moreover, his very real physical and at times political isolation in prison has produced an exaggerated picture of his intellectual isolation while writing the *Notebooks*.[10]

Another difficulty derives from the special weight of Italian culture in his work. By attempting to take account of writers like Machiavelli, Cuoco, De Sanctis and Croce, Gramsci's writings have reference points which are very different from those of traditional Marxism. A specific national tradition is not present in the same way in Marx's texts, the product of the famous triad of German philosophy, English political economy, and French politics. Similarly, it can be argued that there is no particular presence of Russian culture *per se* in Lenin's texts (as differentiated from his object of analysing the Russian concrete situation).[11]

Related to his conditions of work is the fact that Gramsci's notes in prison often have more than one object. Gramsci's literal object is not always his real object. His writings on the Risorgimento, for example, which for many years were the source of an historiographical debate,[12] can be analysed as a discussion of political strategy and as a reflection on the nature of the constituion of the dominance of the bourgeoisie in Italy.[13] Each note uses concepts which are never systematically explained, whose meaning must be deduced from the whole of

Gramsci's work. As a consequence each passage can serve as the raw material for a discussion of several different aspects of Gramsci's thought.

Given these difficulties and given the wide debate which exists about hegemony, which is undoubtedly the key concept in Gramsci's thought, it is impossible to provide a comprehensive discussion in a short essay. We would, however, like to argue against certain misreadings of Gramsci by concentrating on three aspects central to a proper understanding of his problematic.

First of all, it is important to realize that Gramsci develops the concept of hegemony, as he attempts to analyse the state, in a specific historical period, the period of imperialism and the dominance of monopoly capitalism. Thus his analysis of the modern state is part of the task he sets himself of examining the contradictory effects of the development of capitalism and the consequences of this development for the creation of a revolutionary strategy appropriate to the transition to socialism in this historical period. Another crucial aspect of the objects of Gramsci's work is the fact that after 1917 the building of a socialist state is a *concrete* problem and the need to develop Marxist theory to enable it to serve the working class in this new situation was manifest to Gramsci.[14] At the same time the experience of the post-First World War struggle in Western and Central Europe, and the dramatic economic and political crisis of 1929–30, demonstrated the difficulty of maintaining power once the working class had overturned the existing state[15] and, at the same time, showed the ability of the bourgeoisie to re-organize itself politically and economically despite political and economic crises. Any attempt to examine Gramsci's concept of hegemony must take account of the specificity of his object.

A further aspect of Gramsci's work which is important for an understanding of the political basis of hegemony concerns his study of the French Revolution and the Risorgimento, and the political lessons to be drawn from these examples of the bourgeois revolution. As we shall see from these notes, Gramsci's indications for a political strategy for the working class which aims at establishing its hegemony and building an alternative historical bloc are quite complex and do not simply suggest a symmetry between the bourgeois and proletarian revolutions, as Anderson writes.[16] Finally, related to the above and quite relevant to eventual applications of Gramsci's theory to concrete political strategy and tactics, is his discussion of hegemony as a relationship of compromises of a particular nature and within certain limits.

In discussing these features of Gramsci's thought, the inadequacies of certain interpretations should become apparent. More specifically I will implicitly be arguing against a series of often interrelated interpretations which are most common in the Anglo-Saxon literature. Probably the most common of these sees hegemony as legitimization in the Weberian sense, or as 'false consciousness', a process of indoctrination.[17] Although Gramsci is determined to 'unmask' the nature of politics, he is quite outside a problematic which views the working class as a mere *object* of culture and ideas abstracted from the class struggle.[18] Related is an interpretation of hegemony reduced to ideological and cultural activity.[19]

Gramsci's contribution to political theory is consequently reduced. A result of this view has been to present hegemonic intervention by a political party as simply a fight for different ideas and a different culture. This obscures the complexity of determining the *content* of an alternative hegemony, a content which can only be created through a continuous analysis of the nature of the historical bloc maintaining the present social formation, an analysis which in turn determines a political strategy.

Another controversial aspect concerns the *site* of the struggle for hegemony. The difficulty of delineating civil and political society in Gramsci's works has been noted.[20] At the same time there has been a tendency to place the struggle for hegemony in civil society, whereas the state, or political society, understood in a reductive way as the public area of coercion, is given to politics in a narrow sense. We shall discuss this further below, but here we would simply suggest that a useful indication in this regard is provided by Togliatti's comment that in Gramsci's work there is a *methodological* rather than real or substantive difference between the two aspects of a social formation.[21] It is the changing relationship between the state in the narrow sense and society as a whole which is the object of Gramsci's study. Moreover it must be stressed that he never separates force and consent but that he argues that they are always interrelated.[22] The sense in which the different aspects of a single, complex, and contradictory phenomenon, the dominance of a class, which maintains its ability to reconstitute and reproduce itself, and a dominant mode of production, *cannot* be separated is related to precisely the new relationship between society and the state in the modern period.[23]

The 'culturalist' or 'ideologistic' reading of Gramsci is at the root of a criticism of his notion of the state as a 'weak' concept which underestimates the effectiveness of the elements of coercion and the use of force. This view considers Gramsci's concept of the state and its strategic corollary, the war of position, as a product of a period in which the working class is forced to wage a defensive struggle. Gramsci's argument in fact is an attempt to go beyond the dichotomy of defensive or offensive strategies which was the hallmark of the Second International and which remained as the basis for the sudden zigzags of Comintern policy.[24]

The modern state

It is of crucial importance to understand that Gramsci developed his concept of hegemony (and the war of position) with regard to the state in a specific historical conjuncture, that of imperialism and the dominance of finance capital. This is most obvious if his writings in the 1919–20 period are related to a series of notes from prison. In the earlier writings he discusses the crises of the liberal state and the difficulty of the bourgeoisie to guarantee production in this specific historical conjuncture. This is the basis of his argument that the working class has a special opportunity to substitute the bourgeoisie in all its aspects as a ruling class. In the Notebooks, in addition to those passages quite directly related to a discussion of hegemony and the war of position, notes of great relevance – though less frequently discussed – are those on Americanism and Fordism and the passive revolution. These notes consider the contradictory effects of the development and reconstitution of capitalism and imply that the working class must consider each historical moment, however difficult, as an opportunity for a creative, positive political intervention.

Nor should it be forgotten that the concept of hegemony was developed in a period in which the problems of building a socialist state have become concrete after the Russian Revolution, problems which were the subject of wide debates in the Comintern and in the working-class movement in general. It can be argued that it is Gramsci's qualitatively original development of the concept of hegemony, when the word itself was fairly commonly used, which constitutes an attempt to suggest a theoretical basis for the need for a new strategy in advanced capitalist countries, as well as to provide theoretical tools for the building of a socialist state, an historically new task which neither Marx, Engels, nor Lenin would have investigated fully.[25]

What is the period of the modern state, which Gramsci calls the integral or extended state, defined as hegemony fortified by coercion?[26] This state engages in a war of position, argues Gramsci, a strategy developed in the period beginning about 1870. In a passage rich in implications, which illustrates among other things his argument that the war of movement is reduced (but not eliminated) to a *tactical* instance *within* an overall strategy of the war of position, Gramsci discusses the,

Political concept of *the so-called 'Permanent Revolution'*, which *emerged before 1848* as a scientifically evolved expression of the Jacobin experience from 1789 to Thermidor. The formula belongs to an historical period in which *the great mass political parties and the great economic trade unions did not yet exist*, and society was still, so to speak, in a state of fluidity from many points of view: greater backwardness of the countryside, and almost complete monopoly of political and State power by a few cities or even by a single one (Paris in the case of France); *a relatively rudimentary State apparatus, and greater autonomy of civil society from State activity*; a specific system of military forces and of national armed services; greater autonomy of the national economies from the economic relations of the world market, etc. *In the period after 1870, with the colonial expansion of Europe, all these elements change*: the internal and international organisational relations of the State become more complex and massive, and the Forty-Eightist formula of the 'Permanent Revolution' is expanded and transcended in political science by the formula of 'civil hegemony'. The same things happens in the art of politics as happens in military art: war of movement increasingly becomes war of position, and it can be said that a State will win a war in so far as it prepares for it minutely and technically in peacetime. The massive structures of the modern democracies, both as State organisations, and as complexes of associations in civil society, constitute for the art of politics as it were the 'trenches' and the permanent fortifications of the front in the war of position: they render merely 'partial' the element of movement which before used to be 'the whole' of war, etc.[27]

Thus the state is expanded and its relationship to civil society changes in the period of imperialism and the period of the greatest organization of the working class in trade unions and political parties, indeed the period of the growth of mass organizations in general. Moreover, the historical example of the potential of the working class to construct a new type of state, the Paris Commune, is the new 'spectre' haunting Europe. It is a period in which the masses are *in* politics, in which political parties with mass bases are represented in parliaments, whatever the *content* of this participation, for the first time in history. The organization of the masses economically and politically is a necessary thought not a sufficient condition of their fulfilling their role as political subjects. They now have a *potential* for political intervention understood in the sense of a potential for constructing a new society. This potential is hereafter a permanent feature of the concrete situation.[28] At the same time the bourgeois social formation no longer represents the advance of the whole of society, is no longer 'progressive' as it had been in the period of ascendant capitalism.

The context of the new relationship between masses and politics comes to be ignored when the war of position is reduced to a mere defensive strategy applicable to the post-1921 period and the downturn in the revolutionary fortunes of the working-class movement. This reduction of Gramsci's theoretical and strategic indications is in turn related to a specific tactic or policy, in particular the United Front, and the promotion of the New Economic Policy (NEP) in Russia. This interpretation is usally based on a note in which Gramsci wrote:

> It seems to me that Ilitch understood that a change was necessary from the war of manoeuvre applied victoriously in the East in 1917, to a war of position which was the only form possible in the West – where, as Krasnov observes, armies could rapidly accumulate endless quantities of munitions, and where the social structures were of themselves still capable of becoming heavily-armed fortifications. This is what the formula of the 'United Front' seems to me to mean, and it corresponds to the conception of a single front for the Entente under the sole command of Foch . . .
>
> Ilitch, however, did not have time to expand his formula – though it should be borne in mind that he could only have expanded it theoretically, whereas the fundamental task was a national one; that is to say it required a reconnaissance of the terrain and identification of the elements of trench and fortress represented by the elements of civil society, etc.[29]

There follows the passage contrasting East and West, which we shall discuss below. There are two important points to be made, one specific to Gramsci's texts, and one rather more general. This passage can be read in terms of the necessity of understanding the change of policy with regard to a fundamental analysis of the nature of advanced capitalist social formations, rather than a temporary setback in the transition to socialism. While it might have *seemed* as if there was the possibility of using the October model in Western Europe in the post-First World War period, the state was at all times the modern extended state so that at no time in this period of history had the war of movement been adequate as a *strategy*. Gramsci argues:

> Even those military experts whose minds are now fixed on the war of position, just as they were previously on that of manoeuvre naturally *do not maintain that the latter should be considered as expunged from military science*. They merely maintain that, in wars among the more industrially and socially advanced States, *the war of manoeuvre must be considered as reduced to more of a tactical than a strategic function*; that it must be considered as occupying the same position as siege warfare used to occupy in relation to it.
>
> *The same reduction must take place in the art and science of politics, at least in the case of the most advanced States*, where 'civil society' has become a very complex structure and one which is resistant to the catastrophic 'incursions' of the immediate economic element (crises, depressions, etc.). The superstructures of civil society are like the trench-systems of modern warfare. In war it would sometimes happen that a fierce artillery attack seemed to have destroyed the enemy's entire defensive system, whereas in fact it had only destroyed the outer perimeter; and at the moment of their advance and attack the assailants would find themselves confronted by a line of defence which was still effective.
>
> *The same thing happens in politics, during the great economic crises*. A crisis cannot give the attacking forces *the ability to organise* with lightning speed in time and in space; still less can it endow them with fighting spirit. Similarly, the defenders are not demoralised, nor do they abandon their positions, even among the ruins, nor do they lose faith in their own strength or their own future. Of course, things do not remain exactly as they were; but it is certain that one will not find the element of speed, of accelerated time, of the definitive forward march . . .[30]

This in fact constitutes a self-criticism and a critique of all those on the left who thought of the post-First World War period as 'revolutionary' simply because there was a crisis in the political and economic systems. Gramsci in the Notebooks develops the theme from his earlier writings concerning the need for the working class to be able to construct a new state, to affirm itself in this sense as a ruling class. In the earlier writings, in fact up to 1926, this co-existed, we would argue, with a view of the 'revolutionary situation' which does not really succeed in going beyond the before/after dichotomy which was a mark of the problematic of the Second International. But this is another essay. We would simply suggest here that in addition to the development of the concept of hegemony, a crucial aspect of Gramsci's later problematic in this context is his notion of the passive revolution.

The other, more general aspect concerns the relationship of Gramsci's ideas to any concrete policy. Perry Anderson goes to great lengths to reduce what has come to be known as 'Eurocommunism' to the parliamentary road and the peaceful transition to socialism (ignoring among other things the whole debate in Italy and elsewhere about the need to change radically state institutions and to develop new modes of political intervention and to expand democratic control by the masses – a perspective which itself raises a whole set of problems which are now *real* tasks confronting the working-class movement). In turn Anderson implies that this is based on a mistaken, Gramscian view of the state.

This line of argument is faulty on a whole variety of grounds. First of all, it remains to be proved that Gramsci's theory unavoidably leads to the present strategy of these parties. In answering this question, a second one must at least be posed: is it not possible that these strategies can only be understood (and criticized) in terms of mediations with regard to the application of theoretical tools to a qualitatively changed situation, post-Second World War Europe issuing from the anti-fascist struggle. The reconstructed Italian state, for example, as it has emerged from the Resistance and thirty years of class struggle, presents a set of institutions of popular democracy and a constitution which are certainly not the product of the dictates of a single class but rather of the balance of social, political and class forces growing out of the Resistance.

Stemming from this question is another which must also be considered. Keeping to the Italian example, the post-war strategy of the Italian Communist Party (PCI) cannot simply be reduced to the ideas of Gramsci (who was in any case writing in very different circumstances); the contribution of Togliatti and others must also be investigated.[31] The relationship between theoretical tools of analysis, in this case Gramsci's concept of hegemony, and a specific strategy is extremely complex and cannot be broached here. Anderson fails to acknowledge this complexity.[32]

A fundamental aspect of Gramsci's development of the concept of hegemony which Anderson and many other commentators ignore concerns Gramsci's attempt to analyse the new relationship between state and society in the period of the dominance of finance capital. Dealt with most directly in his articles in 1919–20, Gramsci tries to analyse the contradictory consequences of the increased intervention by the state in society in the period of the organization, real or potential, of the masses.[33] In these articles Gramsci discussed the dominance of monopoly capital, a dominance increased by the war, which diminished the role of the individual entrepreneur and of traditional sources of investment and consequently the social and economic role of whole groups of people. The following passage, for example, examines the decline of the economic (and ideological) role of the individual entrepreneur and changes in the role of the state.

> The factory is not an independent entity. It is not run by an owner-entrepreneur who possesses the commercial know-how (stimulated by the interest that is inherent in private ownership) to buy the raw materials wisely and sell the manufactured object at a profit. These functions have been displaced from the individual factory and transferred to the system of factories owned by the same firm. And it does not stop here: *they are concentrated in the hands of a bank or system of banks*, who have taken over real responsibility for supplying raw materials and securing markets for sales.
>
> But during the war, and as a result of the war, was it not the State which supplied raw materials to industry, distributed them in accordance with a pre-established plan and became the sole purchaser of production? *So what has happened to the economic figure of the owner-entrepreneur, the captain of industry*, who is so indispensable to production and who causes the factory to flourish, through his foresight, his initiatives and the stimulus of his own personal interest? This figure has vanished, has been liquidated in the process of development of the instruments of labour, in the process of development of the technical and economic relations that constitute the conditions in which production and work are carried on . . .
>
> The owner of capital has become a dead branch in the field of production. Since he is no longer indispensable and his historical functions have atrophied, he has become a mere police agent; he has placed his 'rights' squarely in the hands of the State, so that it will defend them ruthlessly.
>
> In this way the State has become the sole proprietor of the instruments of labour and has taken over all the traditional functions of the entrepreneur. . . .[34]

Without claiming that Gramsci provides a developed investigation of the role of finance capital, which remains quite rudimentary in these writings,[35] the changes in society and politics – in particular the changed relationship between masses and the state rooted in changes in the economy – are from this early period a permanent preoccupation of Gramsci's work.

Later in the Notebooks, in the context of his notes on Americanism and Fordism and the passive revolution, Gramsci comments on the fact that in countries in which finance capital dominates with different forms of political organization (e.g. Roosevelt's United States, Nazi Germany, and fascist Italy) elements of planning are introduced in an attempt to eliminate the anarchy of the economy. The state's relationship to the economy, along with its intervention in spheres of social organization (e.g. different types of welfare systems), and, related to this, the need to organize masses of people who – particularly in the period following the 1918–14 war – begin to appear as political actors, constitute a substantial change, according to Gramsci, in the traditional limited bourgeois state. Thus the traditional liberal notion of a state removed from the economy, limited to a 'night-watchman' function, and overseeing conflicts which are presented ideologically as reconcilable, was threatened by the very development of capital itself, expressed in a variety of political forms.[36]

The state which has this new role and new relationship to society can only be understood if the dominance of a class is analysed in *all* its aspects, as force plus consent, and if the state is viewed not just as the instrument of force of a class (the classical definition provided by Marx, Engels and Lenin) but as the whole variety of activities in a whole range of sites which enable the social relations of production to be reproduced.[37] Thus not only the Church but institutions such as the courts and schools combine political and 'private' functions. Gramsci explains,

> In my opinion, the most reasonable and concrete thing that can be said about the ethical State, the cultural State, is this: every State is ethical in as much as one of its most important functions is *to raise the great mass of the population to a particular cultural and moral level, a level (or type) which corresponds to the needs of the productive forces for development, and hence to the interests of the ruling classes.* The school as a positive educative function, and the courts as a repressive and negative educative function, are the most important State activities in this sense: but, *in reality, a multitude of other so-called private initiatives and activities tend to the same end – initiatives and activities which form the apparatus of the political and cultural hegemony of the ruling classes.*[38]

At the same time, it must be emphasized that Gramsci's analysis of the crisis of the classical, limited liberal state is related to a key feature of his political theory: the potential protagonism of the masses.[39] In the

modern age the state is transformed because the contradictory effects of
the development of capitalism produce the organization of the masses
which now have a potential for self-government for the first time in
history.[40] Thus, when Gramsci writes with regard to the war of position
'the siege is reciprocal',[41] he is trying to explain the following. The
working class cannot choose the terrain on which to fight, *but* it must
realize that the existence of mass organizations have played a crucial
part in the creation of that terrain. That is, the working-class movement
is forced to engage in a struggle with a specific state, but the present,
extended state has the *form* that it has (that is, force plus hegemony) and
engages in the war of position, using various forms of the passive
revolution, because in the period of imperialism, by organizing these
masses economically the capitalist social formation necessarily
provides the basis for their potential political organization, and
therefore their potential to transform society. Gramsci reaffirms Marx's
statement that capitalism must constantly revolutionize itself and put
old forms, old modes of organization, and old ideas into crisis. Gramsci
notes the contradictory aspects of the necessity to organize the mass of
workers when he writes the following in 1924 when the fascist regime
had begun to eliminate autonomous trade union activity:

> Why, while the trade union has lost ground organizationally under the
> pressure of reaction, has the internal commission instead enlarged its
> organizational sphere? . . . Why do the capitalists and the fascists permit
> such a situation to be created and to persist? For capitalism and for fascism
> it is necessary that the working class be deprived of its historical function of
> leader of the other oppressed classes of the population . . . it is necessary,
> that is, to destroy that organization which is external to the factory and is
> concentrated territorially (trade unions and parties), which exercises a
> revolutionary influence on all the oppressed and takes from the government
> its democratic basis of power. But the capitalists, for industrial reasons,
> cannot want every form of organization destroyed: in the factory discipline
> and a good state of production is only possible if there exists at least a
> minimum of constitutionality, a minimum of consent on the part of the
> workers.[42]

At the political level masses must be organized to provide a social basis
for the state. The *content* of the political organization of the masses may
remain insufficient for the task of substituting the present social formation with another, that is they may be at a certain time incapable of
waging a hegemonic struggle. However, the very presence of the masses
in politics for the first time in history is a precondition for their autonomy.

Thus the extended state is a product of a situation in which the potential of the mass movement is a constant threat. At the same time the ability of the capitalist social formation to represent the social, political and economic advance of society as a whole is increasingly diminished in the period of monopoly capitalism. This is the basis of the crisis of hegemony in which the role of traditional political institutions, in particular parliament and the traditional political parties (which for Gramsci included the PSI), see their roles challenged.[43] As the task of maintaining a semblance of national unity, or in Gramsci's terms a collective will, becomes more difficult, the opportunity and the responsibility of the working class to forge such a unity around an alternative project for the advancement of society becomes greater.

The necessity of the bourgeoisie to reconstitute itself politically and economically, to 'revolutionize' itself in Marx's sense, implies the attempt to maintain the *social base* which is required by the state in this historical period. The various political modes of reconstitution are considered by Gramsci when he discusses Caesarism and the passive revolution. References by Gramsci to such diverse phenomena as reformism and fascism, as well as the Italian Risorgimento in the context of the passive revolution, can be better understood if two common features are highlighted: the attempt to create, maintain or increase a political and social base for the state through satisfying at least some of the corporative demands of various social groups, and the simultaneous introduction of qualitatively new elements in the economic organization of society. We shall return to this below.[44]

It should be clear that this modern, extended state is *not* the state which existed in Russia in 1917. Gramsci specifies that,

> This question (of a more complex civil society and hence the war of position) is posed for the modern States, but not for backward countries or for colonies, where forms which elsewhere have been superseded and have become anachronistic are still in vigour.[45]

The famous passage contrasting the state in the East and the West[46] is *not* simply referring to a geographical difference, as Anderson stresses, but must be placed within the context of the numerous specifications of the modern features of the extended state, particularly mass organizations. Moreover, Gramsci writes that under feudalism, for example, the cohesion of society was not based on hegemony.

In the ancient and mediaeval State alike, centralisation, whether political-territorial or social . . . was minimal. The State was, in a certain sense, a mechanical bloc of social groups . . . within the circle of political-military compression, which was only exercised harshly at certain moments, the subaltern groups had a life of their own, institutions of their own, etc., and sometimes these institutions had State functions which made of the State a federation of social groups with disparate functions not subordinated in any way. . . . The modern State substitutes for the mechanical bloc of social groups their subordination to the active hegemony of the directive and dominant group, hence abolishes certain autonomies, which nevertheless are reborn in other forms, as parties, trade unions, cultural associations.[47]

Moreover it can be argued that the state which Gramsci is analysing is different in certain important respects from the object of writings by Marx, Engels, and Lenin on the state. Rather than an analysis of that state which can be considered the national, political correspondent in different forms of imperialism, the classical Marxist and Leninist discussion of the state is based on the analysis of a situation in which the masses are excluded almost entirely from even the potential of effective political intervention. Certainly the problem in Russia in 1917, where the Duma reflected an attempt to adjust political institutions to the needs of historical and economic development but which existed without mass political or trade union organization, was to create and then maintain a new type of state in which the masses could intervene.

The difficulty, then, of delineating the boundaries between civil and political society is a product, not of any 'slippage' into bourgeois thought as Anderson writes,[48] but of the attempt to grasp the complex reality of this modern state. This is not to say that there are no criticisms to be made in this regard in Gramsci's writings. Certainly in his articles in the *Ordine Nuovo* there are problems in the way in which Gramsci suggests that political forms correspond to changes in the economy. He tends, for example, to underestimate the ability of the bourgeoisie to reconstitute itself politically and economically through fascism and he reduces various political expressions of sections of the bourgeoisie to a single phenomenon.[49] Some of these problems and inadequacies undoubtedly extend into the Notebooks and must be examined critically.[50] But the starting point for such a critical examination must be Gramsci's project of investigating the modes of dominance of the bourgeoisie in this specific historical period and the consequences for a strategy for the working class in the transition to socialism.[51]

Gramsci's discussion of bourgeois revolution

Another controversial point concerns the extent to which Gramsci's concept of hegemony is derived from bourgeois thought and from his study of bourgeois revolutions.[52] The first is indeed an important if extremely complex discussion. It cannot be adequately discussed here, but we would simply suggest that the lines of investigation should be extended to consider the relationship between Gramsci's ideas and those of Sorel. In this context, as Nicola Badaloni so effectively argues,[53] it is not sufficient to demonstrate a similarity of themes to prove an identity or even similarity of content. He maintains that Gramsci is inspired by certain elements from Sorel (e.g. the modes of cohesion of social forces and the problem of a cleavage, breaking through, yet born of, a social formation) and transforms them within a new problematic. This must at least be accepted as possible with regard to Gramsci's relation to other thinkers.[54]

It must also be accepted as a methodological possibility when we consider Gramsci's study of the French Revolution and the Risorgimento. There is an important difference between seeking a model from historical examples and trying to understand what is similar and what is structurally different. Gramsci is quite clear, for instance, that while the technique of passive revolution may be used by the bourgeoisie, it is not appropriate for the proletariat.

> The thesis of the 'passive revolution' as an interpretation of the Risorgimento period, and of every epoch characterised by complex historical upheavals. *Utility and dangers of this thesis.* Danger of historical defeatism, i.e. of indifferentism, since the whole way of posing the question may induce a belief in some kind of fatalism, etc. Yet the conception remains a dialectical one in other words, presupposes, indeed postulates as necessary, a vigorous antithesis which can present intransigently all its potentialities for development. *Hence theory of the 'passive revolution' not as a programme, as it was for the Italian liberals of the Risorgimento, but as a criterion of interpretation . . .*[55]

Moreover he states quite clearly that models cannot simply be transplanted from one context to another.[56]

With regard to Gramsci's discussion of the Risorgimento, some preliminary points must be made. Gramsci is considering the following problem: why was the *form* of bourgeois state in Italy the 'bastard' it was?[57] That is, why did one mode of constitution of the political dominance of the bourgeoisie win out over the possibility of another, specifically a state with an extremely restricted social base, not recognized in a juridico-formal sense by the Vatican or in a real sense by the popular masses. In posing these questions and in discussing the Risorgimento, Gramsci's notes contain a number of implicit assumptions.

First of all, it is assumed that hegemony can be achieved by social and political forces representing a part of a class as well as by classes. The two political groupings in the Risorgimento which he discusses, the moderates and the Republican Partito d'Azione (Action Party), represent different sections of the bourgeoisie.[58] Secondly, there is the assumption that any historical situation is the product of a field of contending social and political forces (not just classes) and that the outcome of the struggle between these forces depends on the political abilities (or failures) of all those in the field.[59] This approach is very much influenced by Lenin's method in *Two Tactics of Social Democracy*. The possibility of various outcomes to any moment of the class struggle depending on the political intervention of the various classes is a crucial aspect of the argument put forward by Lenin and demarcates his concept of political intervention from that dominating the Second International. This is echoed by Gramsci when he writes:

> . . . knowing how to find each time the point of progressive equilibrium (in the sense of one's own programme) is the art of the politician, not of the golden mean, but really of the politician who has a very precise line with a wide perspective of the future.[60]

Finally, there is the assumption that there are different modes of political dominance with greater or lesser degrees of hegemony, with wider or more restricted social bases, the particular mode in any one case being determined by, first, the type of relationship between leaders and led, between intellectuals and masses[61] and, secondly, by the ongoing political activities of the different contending forces.

Certain aspects of Gramsci's discussion of the role of the Jacobins in the French Revolution were certainly relevant to problems of the maintenance of power and the building of a socialist state in the USSR, and for revolutionary strategy in general. It should be noted that Gramsci's use of the term Jacobin changes in the course of his work[62] and comes to stand for a political force which is able to create a strategy corresponding to the needs of the mass of the population and to the requirements of preserving the gains of the revolution,[63] these two dimensions of the struggle being interrelated. How was the revolution to be protected? Gramsci writes:

> The first necessity was to annihilate the enemy forces, or at least to reduce them to impotence in order to make a counter-revolution impossible. The second was to enlarge the cadres of the bourgeoisie as such, and to place the latter at the head of all the national forces; this meant identifying the interests and the requirements common to all the national forces, in order to set these forces in motion and lead them into the struggle, obtaining two results: (a) that of opposing a wider target to the blows of the enemy, i.e. of creating a politico-military relation favourable to the revolution; (b) that of depriving the enemy of every zone of passivity in which it would be possible to enrol Vendée-type armies.[64]

The destruction of the enemy or of its potential to make the counter-revolution depended on the ability of the political leadership of the progressive class to unite the mass of the population in order to create a permanent base for the new state. This unity could only be founded on a concrete political programme based on a correct understanding of the need to build a concrete historical bloc and of the nature of that bloc.

This brings us to Gramsci's comparison of the political intervention of the moderates with the failure of the Partito d'Azione in the Risorgimento and the *political* basis of the struggle for hegemony. A theme which runs through the Notebooks is Gramsci's criticism of what he calls a rationalistic, abstract, and schematic approach to concrete political problems. His aim is to criticize a style of politics going back to the Risorgimento and including the Italian Socialist Party and Bordiga's early leadership of the PCI. It is also one of the reasons he criticizes Trotsky.[65]

The discussion which illustrates Gramsci's position most clearly has to do with the role of religion as the ideological cement binding the mass of the peasantry, preventing their adherence to a more progressive struggle and helping to preserve the political and economic role of the Vatican. The Church in Italy was an important organizer of the intellectuals providing a certain world outlook as well as being a feudal landlord bound in a more direct sense to the preservation of certain socio-economic relations on the land. The Partito d'Azione, for example Mazzini and others, were certainly not short of anti-clerical arguments, but this ideological, cultural struggle was not based, according to Gramsci, on a clear political strategy and a concrete political programme of land reform adhering to the potential of the situation. Gramsci maintained that the religious question could not be solved by propaganda. The political effects of religion as an ideology could only be counteracted through a strategy based on an analysis of the social and economic underpinnings of the ideological and political role of the Vatican.

The only way for the Partito d'Azione to have become the leading political force in the establishment of an Italian nation-state was to have won over the bulk of the population through such a concrete programme. It would thus have been able to prevent the moderates from establishing an historical bloc based on historically conservative forces.

> It is obvious that, in order to counterpose itself effectively to the Moderates, the Action Party ought to have allied itself with the rural masses, especially those in the South, and *ought to have been 'Jacobin' not only in external 'form' in temperament, but most particularly in socio-economic content.* The binding together of the various rural classes, which was accomplished in a reactionary bloc by means of the various legitimist-clerical intellectual strata, could be dissolved, so as to arrive at a new liberal-national formation, only if support was won from two directions: from the peasant masses, by accepting their elementary demands and making these an integral part of the new programme of government; and from the intellectuals of the middle and lower strata, by concentrating them and stressing the themes most capable of interesting them (and the prospect of a new apparatus of government being formed, with the possibilities of employment which it offered, would already have been a formidable element of attraction for them – if that prospect had appeared concrete, because based on the aspirations of the peasantry).[66]

The moderates, Gramsci writes, understood their own task very well.[67] They were able to prevent a land reform thus gaining support from landed interests and creating a nation-state with a very restricted social base in a relatively backward political form.

There are a number of consequences which can be drawn from this discussion. First of all, Gramsci specifically suggests that there are different modes of political intervention appropriate to different social forces and different political groups. For example, the Jacobins had indeed been successful in creating mass support, and their slogans of liberty, equality, and fraternity corresponded to the needs of the situation,[68] but these slogans remain utopian to the extent that the bourgeois social formation remains based on forms of exploitation. In the Risorgimento, the possible mode of hegemony of the moderates, a mode which involved the 'absorption of the enemies élites' and the ability to influence intellectuals based on the membership of the moderates in the economically dominant class,[69] was quite different from that of the Partito d'Azione because of their different positions in society. Gramsci explained that,

> For the Action Party to have become an autonomous force and, in the last analysis, for it to have succeeded at the very least in stamping the movement of the Risorgimento with a more markedly popular and democratic character (more than that perhaps it could not have achieved, given the fundamental premisses of the movement itself), it would have had to counterpose to the 'empirical' activity of the Moderates (which was empirical only in a manner of speaking, since it corresponded perfectly to the objective) an organic programme of government which would reflect the essential demands of the popular masses, and in the first place of the peasantry. To the 'spontaneous' attraction of the Moderates it would have had to counterpose a resistance and a counter-offensive 'organised' according to a plan.[70]

An implication is that they also needed a different form of organization.

Gramsci is also quite explicit about the particular difficulties which the working class faces in establishing its hegemony.

> ... creating a group of independent intellectuals is not an easy thing; it requires a long process, with actions and reactions, coming together and drifting apart and the growth of very numerous and complex formations. It is the conception of a subaltern social group, deprived of historical initiative, in continuous but disorganic expansion, unable to go beyond a certain qualitative level, which still remains below the level of the possession of the State and of the real exercise of hegemony over the whole of society which alone permits a certain organic equilibrium in the development of the intellectual group.[71]

Indeed, Marxism has the very difficult task, he writes, of having both to interact with the masses at their cultural level and to fight the more sophisticated philosophy of the ruling classes.[72] This implies the need for a special kind of hegemonic relationship in the socialist revolution, a democratic, representative relationship.[73]

Gramsci is also quite clear that hegemony before state power is always incomplete and relative. The ability to attain and maintain state power depends on a political force representing the *most* hegemonic element. The achievement of state power presents the possibility of a full development of hegemony so that a class can become truly autonomous and hegemonic.[74]

Referring specifically to the struggle of the working class, Gramsci writes that the *content* of the hegemony of the new state and the *forms* of the superstructure cannot be predetermined. That is, this hegemony is not simply based on the existing culture of the subaltern classes[75] nor are the superstructures simply to be adopted from the past. (This would constitute, after all, a form of passive revolution.) The class struggle produces changes in both the forms and content of hegemony and in the institutions of the superstructure. Coupled with his polemic against empty, rhetorical stances, this argument suggests that the precise content of a struggle for hegemony would depend on the particular conjuncture, and specifically on an analysis of the historical bloc supporting the present social formation.

Hegemony as a relationship of compromises

This brings us to one final point. The hegemony of a class consists in its ability to represent the 'universal' interests of the whole of society and to unite to itself a group of allies. It is a hegemonic intervention which is the only activity which Gramsci qualifies as truly political. In his analysis of the three moments of a relation of political forces, it becomes apparent that it is not the site of the struggle (or the institution) which qualifies an intervention as political or hegemonic but the nature of the intervention itself. Thus, for example, participation in parliament, which involves representing the corporative interests of a class, is not truly political activity of a class.[76] In the truly political phase the struggle is undertaken as a battle between alternative hegemonies, when the interests of a class become the interest of other subordinate groups, when

> . . . the phase in which previously germinated ideologies . . . come into confrontation and conflict, until only one of them, or at least a single combination of them, tends to prevail, to gain the upper hand, to propagate itself throughout society – bringing about not only a unison of economic and political aims, but also intellectual and moral unity, posing all the questions around which the struggle rages not on a corporate but on a 'universal' plane, and thus creating the hegemony of a fundamental social group over a series of subordinate groups.[77]

Consequently it is not the site but the mode of political intervention which qualifies it as truly political. Gramsci continues:

> It is true that the State is seen as the organ of one particular group, destined to create favourable conditions for the latter's maximum expansion. But the development and expansion of the particular group are conceived of, and presented, as being the motor force of a universal expansion, of a development of all the 'national' energies. In other words, the dominant group is coordinated concretely with the general interests of the subordinate groups, and the life of the State is conceived of as a continuous process of formation and superseding of unstable equilibria (on the juridical plane) between the interests of the fundamental group and those of the subordinate groups – equilibria in which the interests of the dominant group prevail, but only up to a certain point, i.e. stopping short of narrowly corporate economic interest.[78]

Thus the state *is* an instrument of a class in its ability to create and reproduce social relations of production, but the *use* of this instrument is qualified by the constantly changing relation of political forces and the compromises which must always be made by the dominant group and a range of allies.[79]

In another note, Gramsci specifies more clearly the relationship of these compromises to the maintenance of a dominant mode of production. Hegemony, he explains, is not simply an ideological struggle unrelated to the sphere of economic relations nor does it imply just any kind of compromises.

> Undoubtedly the fact of hegemony presupposes that account be taken of the interests and the tendencies of the groups over which hegemony is to be exercised, and that a certain compromise equilibrium should be formed – in other words, that the leading group should make sacrifices of an economic-corporate kind. But there is also no doubt that such sacrifices and such compromise cannot touch the essential; for though hegemony is ethical-political, it must also be economic, must necessarily be based on the decisive function exercised by the leading group in the decisive nucleus of economic activity.[80]

What, however, is the nature of these compromises? How do they differ from the compromises (or reforms) instituted by a variety of modes of bourgeois rule which Gramsci describes with the concept of passive revolution?

Now if these passages are related to Gramsci's argument that the passive revolution is not a suitable mode of intervention by the proletariat, it becomes clear that the compromises implied in a hegemonic relationship between the working class and its allies are not simply the result of giving in to the corporative demands of various sectors of the population but of transcending them. This is the crucial difference between the kinds of compromises made by the bourgeoisie and which are a hallmark of social democracy, and those involved in a strategy by the proletariat to transform society. The proletariat can represent the 'universal' expansion of society as a whole only if it is able to unite various sectors around an alternative project which attempts to resolve fundamental problems. The reformism of social democracy and the Welfare State in a number of countries is indeed a response to the class struggle, but the increase in the burden of the state in assuming responsibility for a number of social and economic problems (and giving in to certain corporative demands) without attempting in any serious sense to restructure society in order to overcome the causes of these problems is another aspect of the passive revolution.[81]

This is related to the fact that the utopianism of the bourgeois slogan of 'fraternity' stems precisely from the way in which the capitalist mode of production and the social relations it engenders separates sections of the population. In his early writings Gramsci wrote that the very wage slavery of the worker is expressed in terms of his particular skill and his competition with other workers and with other sections of the population. When Gramsci criticizes the trade unions and the PSI for remaining within bourgeois legality, he is not arguing abstractly in favour of breaking the law. He is criticizing the way in which the corporativism of those organizations implies acceptance of the definition of the worker as a wage slave, separated from other workers and other sections of the population.[82] This corporativism prevents the creation of a strategy able to overcome the bourgeois formal-legal definition of individuals as citizens, unrelated to their social and economic positions. If the working class remains limited within this corporatism, the demands it puts forward and the compromises it makes (or in other words its relations with other classes and groups) cannot form the foundation for a new social bloc, a new type of society.

Thus, the presence of working class organizations *per se*, in state institutions, does not constitute a political intervention by the working class in the full sense unless it is an intervention which is able to unite different social forces going beyond their corporative interests. This is the only way to begin creating an alternative historical bloc and a new state. At the same time the *potential* of a political intervention by the working class conditions the existence of the modern state. This state, to the extent that it must preserve a bloc of forces, can never be viewed simply as an instrument of a class but must be understood as an instrument whose form and use is a product of the compromises necessitated by the class struggle. Yet if these compromises remain on the corporate level, even if they are a product of a militant struggle, the working class remains within the limits of the passive revolution undertaken by the dominant class to perpetuate its rule and to enable it to reproduce the social relations of production. The bourgeoisie is thus able to 'revolutionize' society, as Marx had suggested, reorganizing and changing elements, according to its own plan. What Gramsci calls the 'organic' crisis of capitalism in the age of monopoly capitalism continues without either resolving fundamental problems or resulting in the breakdown of capitalism.[83]

This crisis (and the more dramatic 'conjunctural' crises) provide an ever-changing terrain for the intervention of the working class, an opportunity for a creative, hegemonic role. If the working class does not seize this opportunity, the dominance of the bourgeoisie can be reconstituted in new forms, implying a re-organization of the economy and the maintenance of an historic bloc supporting the existing state.[84] A hegemonic, non-corporative response to the crisis of capitalism is the only way to provide a different type of solution to a crisis which itself is a product of the class struggle and involves all sections of society, a solution which is part of the process of moving society in a socialist direction in a period in which the very crisis of capitalism provides the concrete potential for the transition to socialism.

NOTES

1. See Chantal Mouffe and Anne Showstack Sassoon, 'Gramsci in France and Italy – a Review of the Literature', *Economy and Society*, vol. VI, no. 1, February 1977, for a discussion of some of the literature in this debate. In Italy in the last two years it has involved a discussion about the relationship between socialist pluralism and liberal democracy, between Gramsci's concept of hegemony and the concept of the dictatorship of the proletariat, and about his ideas on the party.
2. See, for example, Giuseppe Vacca in the paper he read in London in March 1977, 'The Political Question of the Intellectuals and the Marxist Theory of the State in the Thought of Gramsci' (at the Gramsci Conference organized by Lawrence and Wishart and the Polytechnic of Central London).

3. The most noteworthy recent example is Perry Anderson's article, 'The Antinomies of Antonio Gramsci', *New Left Review*, no. 100, November 1976–January 1977. A polemical book by Maria Antonietta Macchiocchi does the opposite, claiming that Gramsci's ideas lead to an alternative revolutionary strategy (*Pour Gramsci*, Paris, 1973).

4. In a sense, therefore, these writings should be considered fragments as the notes written in prison obviously are.

5. A note which illustrates his determination to cope with the situation in prison is called 'The Wisdom of the Zulus'. He writes: 'The wisdom of the Zulus has elaborated this maxim reported by an English magazine: "It is better to advance and die than to stop and die."' *Quaderni del carcere*, vol. III, Turin, 1975, p. 1769.

6. What Gramsci wrote about the way in which Marx's works should be treated in a note entitled 'Questions of Method' could well be applied to his own work: 'A distinction should . . . be made within the work of the thinker under consideration between those works which he had carried through to the end and published himself or those which remain unpublished, because incomplete, and those which were published by a friend or disciple . . . It is clear that the content of posthumous works has to be taken with great discretion and caution, because it cannot be considered definitive but only as material still being elaborated and still provisional' (*Selections from the Prison Notebooks*, translated and introduced by Quintin Hoare and Geoffrey Nowell Smith, London, 1970, p. 384; hereafter *Selections*). We might mention that the recent publication of the full text of all the notes Gramsci wrote in prison, in *Quaderni*, op. cit., shows without doubt that the first, post-war edition, prepared under the tutelage of Togliatti (which tended to publish the final version of those notes which had more than one version in the notebooks), was uncensored with the exception of a very few notes which discussed Trotsky. (An example of such a note, cut in the first Italian edition, is paragraph one, *Selections*, p. 236.)

7. Use of the new edition makes it possible to see how often the second draft of a note employed much more obscure language (see the last paragraph of footnote 5, *Selections*, pp. 56–7).

8. A study of Gramsci's writings in the 1923–6 period in which he undertook a debate with Bordiga in the attempt to transform the PCI simply does not sustain Gwyn Williams's attempts to synthesize the two thinkers (*Proletarian Order*, London, 1975). Nor does the undoubted influence of Bordiga on Gramsci in the early years after the founding of the party, discussed by Alastair Davidson, do justice to the way in which Gramsci's criticisms of Bordiga's position, in particular its inherent economism, forms an important element in the development of his ideas (see A. Davidson, *Antonio Gramsci: Towards an Intellectual Biography*, London, 1977. For source material in English on this period see *Selections from Political Writings, 1921–1926*, translated and introduced by Quintin Hoare, London, 1978).

9. The only book in English which deals with this period, Davidson, ibid., does not really discuss Gramsci's ideas in any depth. Books in other languages concentrate on the history of the Italian Communist Party (PCI) in this period.

10. The introduction to *Selections* tends to emphasize Gramsci's isolation, p. lxviii. This view is modified by various testimonials published in Italy which show that while there was a period in which relationships between Gramsci and other

members of the party were tense, he was able to keep in contact with Togliatti and others and with the situation in the world at large through various intermediaries, including Piero Sraffa. A recent book by Paolo Spriano, which examines the evidence available in true detective fashion, refutes the testimonial by Gramsci's brother Gennaro to Fiori (in Giuseppe Fiori, *Antonio Gramsci: Life of a Revolutionary*, London, 1970), arguing that there is simply no concrete evidence of a split between Gramsci and the PCI although he did not agree with the Third Period policy (Spriano, *Gramsci in carcere e il partito*, Rome, 1977; to be published in English by Lawrence and Wishart as *Antonio Gramsci and the Party: The Prison Years*).

11. The differences between Russian and Western Marxism enjoys a wide literature of course from the 1920s or even earlier.

12. For a summary of this debate see John M. Cammett, 'Two Recent Polemics on the Character of the Italian Risorgimento', *Science and Society*, vol. XXVII, no. 4, Fall, 1963, and his appendix, 'Gramsci and the Risorgimento', in *Antonio Gramsci and the Origins of Italian Communism*, Palo Alto, 1967.

13. We discuss this point further below.

14. This is another point made in Vacca's paper, op. cit.

15. The problem of maintaining state power and of constructing a new society as the most difficult aspect of the revolution goes back to Gramsci's earlier writings where the examples of Hungary, Bavaria and other experiences posed it dramatically. See for example, *Selections from Political Writings, 1910–1920*, introduced by Quintin Hoare and translated by John Mathews, London, 1977, p. 306.

16. Anderson, op. cit., p. 20.

17. Ralph Miliband's *State in Capitalist Society*, London, 1969, explicitly reduces hegemony to legitimization while Carl Boggs's *Gramsci's Marxism*, London, 1976, considers hegemony as the maintenance of false consciousness.

18. See Christine Buci-Glucksmann's criticism of Nicos Poulantzas in this respect in her *Gramsci et l'état*, Paris, 1974, pp. 75–6.

19. This is related to the criticism of Gramsci's theory of the state as a 'weak' and naïve view of politics. See below. It could be argued that the basis of Anderson's discussion of hegemony is in fact this kind of reduction.

20. Anderson discusses this at length. See also introduction to the section on 'State and Civil Society' in *Selections*, pp. 206–9.

21. See 'Leninism in the Thought and Action of A. Gramsci', by Togliatti which is included in a selection of his works edited by Donald Sassoon to be published by Lawrence and Wishart. The article is discussed in Mouffe and Showstack Sassoon, op. cit.

22. This tendency to attempt to separate the two aspects is very widespread in the Anglo-Saxon literature on Gramsci (for a useful bibliography of this, see Phil Cozens, *Twenty Years of Antonio Gramsci*, London, 1977).

23. The 'either/or dichotomy' is implicit in the words which are used by Anderson: 'preponderance', 'oppositions', 'counterpose', 'primacy'.

24. Gramsci in fact reduces the war of movement to a tactic within a strategy of war of position which, he says, is the only definitive struggle. See for example, *Selections*, pp. 242–3, which is discussed below. Anderson's comparison of the Gramscian problematic to Kautsky's discussion of the war of attrition and the various positions within German social democracy misses the essential point that the whole

of the discussion in the Second International revolved around alternative strategies, with an implicit or an explicit assumption of *either* one *or* the other related to a crisis theory of the downfall of capitalism. The extent to which this persisted in the Comintern in the 1920s and Gramsci's attempt to suggest an alternative is discussed in *Selections*, the footnote on p. 169, with reference to Gramsci's note, 'Prediction and Perspective'.

25. As Anderson points out the actual word was used extensively in the Russian Social Democratic Labour Party early in the century to indicate the influence of the working class over other classes. Christine Buci-Glucksmann, op. cit., discusses how it was used by people like Bukharin and Stalin in the 1920s and how Gramsci's concept in the Notebooks differed. Until 1926 and his essay on the Southern question Gramsci applied the term 'hegemony' exclusively to the leadership by the proletariat in a set of alliances. Although as Buci-Glucksmann writes there are 'practical' elements born of the political practice of the *Ordine Nuovo* group in this early period which contribute to a more developed concept of hegemony, it is not until the Notebooks that the concept is extended fully to the mode of constitution of the bourgeoisie as a ruling class in the modern period. This is the original aspect of Gramsci's concept which then provides a theoretical basis for a counter-strategy by the proletariat appropriate to the new political forms of monopoly capital and the construction of a socialist state.

26. *Selections*, p. 263.

27. *Selections*, pp. 242–3. My emphasis throughout.

28. In a note discussing the passive revolution and the war of 1914–18 as an historical break Gramsci writes: 'It is enough to think of the importance which the trade-union phenomenon has assumed, a general term in which various problems and processes of development, of differing importance and significance, are lumped together (parliamentarism, industrial organization, democracy, liberalism, etc.), but which objectively reflects the fact that a new social force has been constituted, and has a weight which can no longer be ignored, etc.' (*Selections*, p. 106).

29. *Selections*, pp. 237–8 (see also *Quaderni*, op. cit., p. 1229). From an historical point of view Gramsci's relation to the United Front policy is quite complex (see introduction, *Selections*, pp. xlvii ff.). In a series of letters from Moscow and Vienna when he finally fully opposed Bordiga's position, Gramsci argued that the development of capitalism in the West had created a much more complex situation which required a much more complicated strategy, a strategy *not* rooted in a specific defeat or series of defeats of the working-class movement but which was made necessary by the different nature of the state. This approach is developed more fully in prison and demonstrates how the debate with Bordiga marks an important moment in the development of Gramsci's thought. It is also noteworthy that at the very time when the discussion in the Comintern about the united front policy revolved around the presumed stabilization of capitalism, Gramsci was already discussing it as a policy adapted to the very nature of the state in advanced capitalist countries. Yet he too retained the Comintern outlook at least until his years in prison, as the Theses of Lyons (1926), which use the terminology of stabilization, demonstrate (for source material on this period and on the debate with Bordiga; including the Lyons Theses, see *Selections from Political Writings, 1921–1926*, op. cit.).

30. *Selections*, pp. 234–5 (my emphasis).

31. Togliatti, for example, definitely goes beyond Gramsci in his ideas of 'il partito nuovo', the mass party of the post-war period, as well as, for instance, in his discussion of the role of political parties and other political forces.

32. Macciocchi does this too but from a different political position (see note 3 above).

33. The subject of the interventionist state was not novel. Bukharin as well as a number of social theorists were concerned with it. The effects of mass organization similarly provided the object of numerous studies, cf. Robert Michels, *Political Parties*, London, 1915, and M. Ostrogorsky, *Democracy and the Organization of Political Parties*, London, 1902.

34. *Selections from Political Writings, 1910–1920*, p. 165 (my emphasis). Gramsci elaborated this further as part of an argument against Tasca's interpretation (see ibid., p. 297).

35. An interesting article which criticizes the lack of development of a theory of finance capital by Italian communists in the period of fascism is by Emilio Sereni, 'Fascismo, capitale finanziario e capitalismo monopolistico di stato nelle analisi dei comunisti italiani', in *Critica marxista*, no. 5, 1972. One of the most important studies of finance capital was written by Pietro Grifone while in prison, *Il capitale finanziario in Italia*, Rome, 1945 (new edition, Turin, 1971), and it can be argued that both Gramsci's writings and Togliatti's *Lectures on Fascism*, London, 1976 constitute a major contribution.

36. This kind of state of course never existed in Italy whereas in Germany the state always sought to protect a weak industrial sector with a variety of interventionist policies. Gramsci is in fact criticizing the ideal of such a state held by various Italian social reformers, such as Salvemini who sought to solve the problems of the South through the institution of free trade. It is this myth of the establishment of a limited liberal state, and its assumption that the political can be separated from the economic sphere, an assumption implicit in a number of ideologies (see note 42), which Gramsci criticizes as completely inappropriate to the problems and possibilities posed by concrete historical development.

37. It should be noted that Gramsci uses both a narrow and an extended definition of the state. With regards to the former (the state as force or defined as government) he almost always prefaces his usage with adjectives such as 'common' or 'restricted' to indicate that he is referring to the most usual if incorrect use of the word.

38. *Selections*, p. 258 (my emphasis). With regard to Anderson's discussion of parliament, he fails to take account of the crisis of the legislative institutions in a variety of countries or the crisis of their ideological function, manifested in part by widespread popular apathy and a 'knownothing' attitude equating all political forces. Perhaps a study of the combined coercive/ideological function of parliament as it exists today could be profitably undertaken using some of Gramsci's indications.

39. It is interesting to note that his definition of a proletarian as opposed to a bourgeois revolution is that the former is expansive, providing for the protagonism of the masses. This is a theme running through his various articles on the Russian Revolution in *Selections from Political Writings, 1910–1920*, op. cit., pp. 28 ff.

40. The assumption underlying this argument is that the masses can only intervene if they are organized. This appears in various places in Gramsci's work, and is an important aspect of his argument in favour of the factory councils which appear in

the post-First World War period to be the form of organization best able to unify and organize the mass of workers outside the Italian Socialist Party (PSI) or the trade union movement. Far from being a result of a spontaneist problematic, these writings reflect Gramsci's concern that the proletariat is not prepared for its historical task and that traditional forms of organization must be augmented if the whole potential of the mass movement is to be realized. For examples see *Selections from Political Writings, 1910–1920*, op. cit., pp. 65, 177–8, 267.

41. *Selections*, p. 239.

42. *La costruzione del partito comunista, 1923–26*, Turin, 1971, p. 6. Togliatti takes account of the ability of the fascist regime to organize hitherto unorganized masses in his *Lectures on Fascism*, op. cit. The way in which this consent and this organization at the level of the factory is related to the introduction of elements of planning and to the exercise of hegemony (that is, the roots of hegemony in changes in the economy) are more fully examined in notes on Americanism and Fordism (see *Selections*, pp. 277–316).

43. There is a large literature in academic political science concerning the crisis of legislatures with respect to executive branches. Recent interest in so-called neo-corporatism also reflects the difficulties of political parties and parliaments as representative institutions.

44. Gramsci specifically differentiates modern forms of what he calls Caesarism from other forms of dictatorship by the fact that it develops when there are mass organizations (see *Selections*, pp. 220–1).

45. *Selections*, p. 243.

46. 'In Russia the state was everything, civil society was primordial and gelatinous; in the West, there was a proper relation between state and civil society, and when the state trembled a sturdy structure of civil society was at once revealed. The state was only an outer ditch, behind which there stood a powerful system of fortresses and earthworks: more or less numerous from one state to the next, it goes without saying – but this precisely necessitated an accurate reconnaissance of each individual country' (*Selections*, p. 238).

47. *Selections*, footnote p. 54. It is true that Gramsci does not discuss the absolutist state here, and our argument is not that the tsarist state in 1917 is adequately described as feudal, but simply that Gramsci is quite aware of the differences between various historical forms of state.

48. See for example Anderson, op. cit., p. 25.

49. Franco De Felice points out that Gramsci tends to equate the various political forces represented by such people as Nitti or Giolitti with reaction and hence with fascism and that he shares in this sense an extremist bent with Bordiga in underestimating the differences between the various responses to the crisis (*Serrati, Bordiga, Gramsci e il problema della rivoluzione in Italia, 1919–1920*, Bari, 1971). This book and other works by De Felice develop the theme of the new relationship between state and society in the modern period.

50. For example the terminology depicting political parties as the 'nomenclature of a class', which appears both in his earlier and his later work, does not really explain the way in which parties represent classes or sections of classes. At the same time Gramsci has a clear idea of the various features of the fascist party as a movement and as a party which cannot be reduced to a single aspect (see *Selections*, pp. 166–7).

51. The way in which liberalism 'thinks' a separation between politics (the limited state) and economics is the basis of the comparison Gramsci makes between liberalism and various forms of economism which are unable to pose the question of the relationship between economics and politics in a way which is adequate to the changes taking place in modern society (see *Selections*, pp. 158 ff.).

52. This is the basis of several of Anderson's criticisms.

53. Nicola Badaloni, *Il marxismo di Gramsci*, Turin, 1975.

54. Anderson does not really consider this possibility when he discusses the influence of Croce on Gramsci. Gramsci is certainly not the only Marxist to take elements from other traditions of thought. Inspired by Lenin, Mao's writings on military strategy, for example, use elements from Clausewitz as well as from classical Chinese military theory.

55. *Selections*, p. 114 (my emphasis). See also *Selections*, p. 232, where he discusses fascist techniques in this respect.

56. See for example his criticism of Giuseppe Ferrari, a figure in the Risorgimento (*Selections*, p. 65).

57. *Selections*, p. 90.

58. For an explanation of the history of these groups see *Selections*, p. 57, footnotes.

59. 'The Risorgimento is a complex and contradictory historical development, which is made an integral whole by all its antithetical elements, by its protagonists and its antagonists, by their struggles, by the reciprocal modifications which these very struggles determine and also by the function of passive and latent forces like the great agricultural masses, as well as, naturally, the function stemming from international relations' (*Quaderni*, p. 961, op. cit.).

60. *Quaderni*, ibid., p. 1825. For an interesting comparison of the views on political intervention of Lenin, Gramsci, and Togliatti, see Franco Calamandrei, 'L'iniziativa politica del partito rivoluzionario da Lenin a Gramsci a Togliatti', in *Critica marxista*, vol. V, no 4–5, July–October 1967.

61. Gramsci writes, for example: 'In order to analyse the socio-political function of the intellectuals, it is necessary to recall and examine their psychological attitude towards the fundamental classes which they put into contact in the various fields. Do they have a "paternalistic" attitude towards the instrumental classes? Or do they think they are an organic expression of them? Do they have a "servile" attitude towards the ruling classes, or do they think that they themselves are leaders, an integral part of the ruling classes?' (*Selections*, p. 97). What he calls the 'mode of existence of the intellectuals' is discussed by Vacca in his paper (see note 2).

62. See *Selections*, pp. 65 ff., for a discussion of different uses of the term. A reading of Gramsci's early writings, which portray Jacobinism as an authoritarian mode of revolution, must be compared with his later use of the term which is quite different. In the Notebooks, we find an examination of the differentiated nature of various bourgeois revolutions and a new understanding of the role of the party so that the key feature of Jacobinism in the positive sense for Gramsci in these writings is the ability of a political force to create a collective will based on the mass of the population, whatever the social base of that mass. An element which remains from Gramsci's earlier writing is a criticism of utopianism. See below.

63. *Selections*, p. 78.

64. *Selections*, pp. 78–9.

65. 'With respect to the "Jacobin" slogan [permanent revolution] formulated in 1848–49, its complex fortunes are worth studying. Taken up again, systematized, developed, intellectualized by the Parvus-Bronstein [Trotsky] group, it proved inert and ineffective in 1905, and subsequently. It had become an abstract thing, belonging in the scientist's cabinet. The [Bolshevik] tendency which opposed it in this literary form, and indeed did not use it "on purpose", applied it in fact in a form which adhered to actual, concrete, living history, adapted to the time and the place; as something that sprang from all the pores of the particular society which had to be transformed; as the alliance of two social groups [i.e. proletariat and peasantry] with the hegemony of the urban group. In one case, you had the Jacobin temperament without an adequate political content; in the second, a Jacobin temperament and content derived from the new historical relations, and not from a literary and intellectualistic label' (*Selections*, pp. 84–5n.).

66. *Selections*, p. 74 (my emphasis).

67. *Selections*, p. 108.

68. *Selections*, p. 78.

69. *Selections*, pp. 59–60.

70. *Selections*, p. 61.

71. *Selections*, pp. 395–6.

72. *Selections*, pp. 395–6. Gramsci discusses this in relation to the function of the mechanistic view of Marxism in the Second International.

73. Gramsci discusses the need for an organic relationship between the intellectuals and the masses in which the intellectuals both understand rationally and *feel* the basic needs of the people. This, he says, is the only way to overcome the division between leaders and led, to create an historical bloc (*Quaderni*, op. cit., pp. 1505–6).

74. See Gramsci's discussion, *Selections*, pp. 397–8.

75. Alastair Davidson's chapter on Sardinia gives an idea of the cruelty and primitiveness of society on the island and helps to explain Gramsci's lack of sentimentality towards folklore (op. cit.). Another very effective portrayal of Sardinian peasant life, which gives a similar picture even though it is set in post-Second World War Italy, is the film by the Taviani brothers, *Padre Padrone*.

76. Gramsci says the first level of political consciousness is an awareness of solidarity among a trade or profession while a second involves an economic class consciousness. 'Already at this juncture,' he writes, 'the problem of the State is posed – but only in terms of winning political-juridical equality with the ruling groups: the right is claimed to participate in legislation and administration, even to reform these – but within the existing fundamental structures' (*Selections*, p. 181).

77. *Selections*, pp. 181–2.

78. *Selections*, p. 182.

79. In a note rich in implications Gramsci discusses how a rigid aversion to compromises is rooted in economism, in which, 'Destruction is conceived of mechanically, not as destruction/construction'. He ends the notes explaining that, 'An appropriate political initiative is always necessary to liberate the economic thrust from the dead weight of traditional policies – i.e. to change the political direction of certain forces which have to be absorbed if a new, homogeneous politico-historical bloc, without internal contradictions, is to be successfully formed. And, since two "similar" forces can only be welded into a new organism either through a series of compromises or by force of arms, either by binding them

to each other as allies or by forcibly subordinating one to the other, the question is whether one has the necessary force, and whether it is "productive" to use it. If the union of two forces is necessary in order to defeat a third, a recourse to arms and coercion (even supposing that these are available) can be nothing more than a methodological hypothesis; the only concrete possibility is compromise. Force can be employed against enemies, but not against a part of one's own side which one wishes rapidly to assimilate, and whose "good will and enthusiasm one needs"' (*Selections*, p. 168).

80. *Selections*, p. 161.

81. An example common to the Western world is the way employment of those already in jobs has, in the main, been protected in the current crisis, while certain categories such as the youth, blacks, or women are in different measures dependent on government assistance without there being any significant attempt to restructure the economy to provide jobs for all those seeking them. The working-class movement has not often been able to suggest a programme adequate to the needs of the mass of the population going beyond the corporate demands of various sectors. Because of the lack of objective unity around an alternative political proposal, various governments are able to play off one group against the corporate demands of another.

82. See for example, *Selections from Political Writings, 1910–1920*, op. cit., pp. 104–5, and pp. 110–11. Gramsci writes: 'Trade unionism . . . organizes workers not as producers, but as wage-earners, i.e. as creatures of the capitalist, private property regime, selling the commodity labour. Trade unionism combines workers on the basis of the tools they use or the material they transform; in other words, trade unionism combines workers on the basis of the form that the capitalist regime, the regime of economic individualism, impresses on them. The use of one tool rather than another, and the transformation of one material rather than another, brings to light different capacities and attitudes to work and to earnings; the worker becomes fixed in his particular capacity and attitude, and sees his job not as a moment of production, but simply as a means of earning a living' (p. 110).

83. This tension between the ability of the capitalist social formation to survive notwithstanding the potential of the working class to create a new society delineates the main features of the transition to socialism in the present period. This is what Gramsci is indicating when he writes: 'The concept of "passive revolution" must be rigorously derived from the two fundamental principles of political science: 1. that no social formation disappears as long as the productive forces which have developed within it still find room for further forward movement; 2. that a society does not set itself tasks for whose solution the necessary conditions have not already been incubated, etc.' (*Selections*, p. 106). This is a paraphrase from Marx's Preface to *The Critique of Political Economy* (ibid., p. 106n).

84. The importance of the passive revolution as an analytical tool was stressed at several papers presented at the 1977 Gramsci conference in Florence. See for example Christine Buci-Glucksmann, 'Sui problemi politici della transizione: classe operaia e rivoluzione passiva'; Franco De Felice, 'Rivoluzione passiva, fascismo, americanismo in Gramsci'; and Giuseppe Vacca, 'La "quistione politica degli intellettuali" e la teoria marxists dello Stato nel pensiero di Gramsci' (a later version of the paper presented in London; see note 2 above) in Istituto Gramsci, *Politica e storia in Gramsci I*, Rome, 1977. The possibility of using the passive revolution as a tool to analyse Stalinism is a theme in several of the papers.

BOB JESSOP

MARX AND ENGELS ON
THE STATE

It is a commonplace that Marx did not produce an account of the state
to match the analytical power of his critique of capitalism in *Das
Kapital*. Indeed, although this great work was to have included an
extended treatment of the state, Marx did not succeed in committing it
to paper. Instead his legacy in this respect comprises an uneven and
unsystematic collection of philosophical reflections, journalism,
contemporary history, political forecasts, and incidental remarks. It
was left to Engels to develop a more systematic account of the origins
and nature of the state and to discuss the general relations between state
power and economic development. However, whilst it was Engels
rather than Marx who first adumbrated a class theory of the state, the
'General' was no more successful than Marx himself in developing this
insight into a complete and coherent analysis of the capitalist state.

But this commonplace should not be taken to imply that Marx made
no lasting contribution to political analysis. On the contrary it is as
much for his theory of proletarian revolution as for his critique of
political economy that Marx merits his eponym and continues to have
an exceptional posthumous influence. Likewise Engels is as well known
for his work on the state and politics as he is for his indictment of early
English capitalism or his philosophy of 'scientific socialism'. In this
respect it is worth noting that, although Lenin, Trotsky, and Gramsci
also failed to produce a systematic analysis of the capitalist state, their
contributions to Marxism are nonetheless heavily weighted towards
political analysis and revolutionary practice. Accordingly it is most
unfortunate that the rich and varied work of these five leading Marxists
(and others) on the state and political power has still to be elaborated
and transformed into a coherent theoretical analysis. Such a task is
clearly beyond the scope of the present paper but some first steps can be
taken in relation to the work of Marx and Engels.

The early Marx

Since the publication of the 1844 manuscripts in 1927 there has been a lively debate among Marxists and Marxologists alike concerning whether or not Marx effected (or experienced) a radical break during the course of his intellectual development. This debate is generally focused on the basic epistemological and philosophical presuppositions of the *1844 Manuscripts* and *Das Kapital* and it has been much complicated by the still more recent republication in 1953 of the hitherto almost ignored *Grundrisse*. But it is also concerned with the relative continuity or discontinuity of Marxian concepts and principles of explanation in the analysis of specific topics in the domains of economics, politics, and ideology. That the two levels of this debate are closely related can be seen particularly clearly in the present context from the Hegelian reading of Marx rendered by Avinieri.* For he seeks to establish the deep-seated continuity of the social and political thought of Marx by tracing the themes of his early work on Hegel's political philosophy through the vicissitudes of Marx's subsequent theoretical development. It is beyond the scope of this paper to discuss the general issues involved in this debate but it is essential for us to confront the particular question of continuity in the Marxian analysis of politics.

This question is overlain by another. For there is also a major dispute concerning whether the Marxian analysis of politics is an original theoretical product or is largely borrowed from the works of Machiavelli, Montesquieu, and Rousseau. Thus Colletti argues that Marx had already developed a near definitive theory of state power before the *1844 Manuscripts* started him on the long march to his most important theoretical discoveries. In particular Colletti argues that the *Critique of Hegel's Philosophy of Law* (1843) and the *Introduction* to a projected revision of that critique (written in 1843–4) embody a mature theory which neither the older Marx, Engels, nor Lenin would improve upon in the least substantially. And he also argues that this so-called mature Marxist theory was heavily indebted to Rousseau for its critique of parliamentarism, the theory of popular delegation, and the need for the ultimate suppression of the state itself. From this Colletti concludes that the originality of Marxism must be sought in the field of social and economic analysis rather than in its politics.[1]

* See p. 67 for Bibliography.

In contrast Blackburn has argued that the real focus of the work of Marx and Engels was political rather than philosophical or economic and that their decisive contribution was the theory of proletarian revolution. And he insists most strongly that in no field has Marxism been more original than in political theory and that Marxists either discovered or thoroughly reworked every important political concept. For the historical materialist concepts of class, party, revolution, bureaucracy, state, nation, etc., are not in the least anticipated in the work of earlier political theorists and philosophers. This leads Blackburn to a different periodization of the development of Marxian political analysis. Thus, whereas Colletti finds a mature and near-definitive theory in the 1843 *Critique*, Blackburn argues that Marx did not even commit himself in outline to the proletarian revolution until 1844 (in the *Introduction*) and was still employing political concepts that were 'spare and rudimentary' in the *Communist Manifesto* some four years later. And, although Marx and Engels were able to develop these concepts through their involvement in the First International, their intervention in the development of the German workers' movement, and their observation of French politics (especially the Paris Commune), they could not – according to Blackburn – complete their theory of proletarian revolution even if they were able to distinguish it from Blanquism and 'democratic faith in miracles'. Blackburn concludes that it was not until the events of 1905 and 1917 that other revolutionary Marxists could substantially (albeit not finally) accomplish this task.[2]

What evidence can be adduced for these radically different views of the trajectory followed by Marx in developing his political theory? In the rest of this paper I shall argue that the evidence is far from consistent and unambiguous because neither Marx nor Engels presented a definitive analysis of the state and politics. Instead we find a wide variety of themes and approaches which are capable of independent (and in part contradictory) theoretical development but which are typically combined in various ways by Marx and Engels in their empirical studies of particular societies and political conjunctures. These themes and approaches occasionally receive an exclusive and one-sided treatment, but they are generally articulated in a way that ensures their mutual qualification in a state of theoretical tension. However, it is also true that we can trace a gradual transformation of these different elements and the manner of their combination so that the

Marxian theory of the state and politics undergoes substantial development from the 1840s to the 1880s. It remains ill-formulated and inconsistent throughout its development but the final version is much more adequate theoretically. But, before presenting our reconstruction of the final Marxian theory, let us first consider the early political writings.

The *Critique of Hegel's Philosophy of Law* is the central work of political theory written by Marx in the period before he became a communist. It is mainly concerned with a criticism of Hegel's method of dialectical logic rather than with a direct examination of Hegel's doctrine of the state. Marx first shows how this method results in an apologia for the Prussian constitution and system of government on the thoroughly idealist grounds that it is the 'empirical existence of the truth', the self-incarnation of God in the world.[3] He then proceeds to examine Hegel's own prescriptions concerning the mediation between the separate spheres of state and civil society to be effected through the monarchy, the executive, and the legislative assembly. It is here that Marx develops a general critique of the separation of the state and civil society and argues that this separation cannot be resolved either through the rule of a neutral bureaucracy or the election of a legislative assembly to govern in the interests of the people.[4]

Thus, although Marx agrees with Hegel that there are two distinct spheres in modern society and that civil society is a sphere of egoism or self-interest, he also denies that this separation is immanent or inevitable and that the state can transcend the war of each against all and secure the common interest of all its citizens. In opposition to the claim that the institutional separation of the state is the logical complement to the self-particularization of the universal Idea, Marx argues that the state becomes fully differentiated only in definite historical circumstances which he identifies mainly in terms of freedom of exchange in commerce and landed property.[5] And, whereas Hegel claims that the bureaucracy in the modern state is a 'universal class' whose necessary and objective function it is to realize the 'universal interest', Marx argues that the egoism of civil society implies that any concept of a 'universal interest' is necessarily a pure abstraction.[6] Nor does the agreed fact that the state assumes an independent material form mean that it can therefore transcend the generalized particularism of civil society. Instead the state itself becomes shot through with class materialism and the bureaucracy simply becomes one particular interest among others. Indeed Marx notes that the various independent groups in Prussian civil society struggle to maintain their interests against the encroachments of the bureaucracy but also need the latter to act as the guarantor of their interests against other groups. In turn the officials tend to appropriate state power as their private property and employ it to further both their corporate and individual interests.[7] Moreover, because state power is used to protect the rights of property (especially those of the Junker class), the Prussian state actually functions to reproduce the war of each against all in civil society.[8] Accordingly the citizens of the modern state are involved in an alienated and estranged form of public life since its constant penetration by private egoism ensures that the universal interest remains abstract and illusory.[9]

Nor can the introduction of a recharged organic feudal order with representation based on estates or, indeed, the further development of the bourgeois democratic republic based on universal suffrage, overcome this estrangement through the reintegration of the public and private lives of the citizens. For, in opposition to Hegel's constitutional prescription that each social class be legally incorporated as a basis for political representation and the fusion of the public and private spheres, Marx argues that this would involve the refeudalization of modern society and destroy the individual freedoms and formal equality of private citizens.[10] He also argues that such estates or corporations would not materially represent the universal interest but would simply reproduce the antagonisms of civil society inside the state.[11] In addition Marx criticizes Hegel's proposals for the popular election of deputies on the twin grounds that they would use their public office to further private interests and that they would dominate rather than represent the people.[12] This means that the parliamentary republic is necessarily limited as a form of popular control because it is inserted into a state whose claim to represent the interest of all its citizens must remain illusory as long as civil society is dominated by the egoism engendered by private property and competition. Thus, if real democracy and the universal interest are to be realized, private property and the abstract state must be abolished.

These themes are elaborated by Marx in his contemporary essay *On the Jewish Question*. This is a critique of the ideas of Bruno Bauer regarding Jewish emancipation and compares the nature and effects of religious and political emancipation. Marx argues that the modern state abolished the political significance of religion, birth, rank, education and occupation through the institution of formal equality among its

citizens; but it could not abolish their continuing social significance.
Thus, although the modern state and civil society are structurally
distinct, it is the egoism of civil society that shapes political activity.[13]
Accordingly Marx concludes that the emancipation of man requires
more than the concession of formal political freedom. It can be
completed only when the individual activities of men are reorganized to
give full expression to their social and public nature.[14]

This stress on human emancipation is articulated with the class
struggle for the first time in the *Introduction to A Contribution to the
Critique of Hegel's Philosophy of Law*. In this brief essay Marx discusses the uneven development of philosophy and society in Germany
and argues that complete emancipation is possible only on the basis of a
proletarian revolution. For, since the nascent proletariat is subject to all
the evils of modern society, it can only achieve its own emancipation
through the total elimination of all exploitation and oppression.[15]
Moreover, given the wholly miserable conditions in which the
proletariat lives, all that is required for the German revolution to occur
is the widespread diffusion of the critical philosophy of the whole man.[16]
In short, whilst the proletariat has nothing to lose but its chains, it
stands to gain the whole world not just for itself but for mankind in
general.

We are now in a position to assess the contributions of the young
Marx to the analysis of politics and the state. It should be apparent that
these studies do not amount to a near-definitive theory of state power
and, indeed, since they take the form of critiques and are very much
preliminary analyses, it is unreasonable to expect them to do so. At best
they reproduce and elaborate certain elements of anti-statism current at
the time and also present a series of acute observations on the nature of
bureaucratic rule and political representation. In this respect it should
be noted that, although these ideas clearly owe much to the work of
other radical liberal democrats, the young Marx locates them in a
problematic which is inspired by Hegel rather than Rousseau. In
addition to his analyses of the modern state Marx also examines the
question of revolution. His emphasis on the role of the proletariat in this
context is more original but its initial presentation is still much
influenced by the Hegelian problematic. Indeed, since Marx had not yet
developed the fundamental concepts of historical materialism, it is
difficult to see how these studies could seriously be described as works
of mature Marxism.

Thus the entire theoretical discussion is cast in a philosophical framework and many of the key economic and political concepts are imbued with heavy philosophical overtones. For, not only are class differences assimilated to those of rank, religion, and education and discussed in terms of an undifferentiated and non-specific conception of private property and human egoism, the relation between the state and civil society is analysed mainly in terms of such oppositions as 'universal-particular' and 'real-abstract'. Likewise the proletariat is seen largely as an underclass (even a lumpen-class) precipitated in the course of a general social disintegration, and its emancipation is seen in terms of the final liberation and fulfilment of an essentially social man who has previously lived in conditions of unfreedom and/or self-estrangement.[17] It is certainly true that Marx consistently argues that this final stage in human emancipation requires the abolition of private property and the abstract state and the introduction of social co-operation and true democracy. But he does not attempt to delineate the future society nor to specify how the transition will be effected. In short a careful reading of these early studies does not support the claim that they contain an elaborate and adequate theory of the modern state and the dynamics of proletarian revolution. Their significance for Marxism in this respect is almost wholly prospective and, had Marx died in 1844, they would merit no special attention today.

Towards a class theory of the state

In general the earliest theoretical work of Marx treats the state as an irrational abstract system of political domination which denies the social nature of man and alienates him from genuine involvement in public life. It also sees the state elite as the representative of private interests and, indeed, argues that the bureaucracy attempts to appropriate state power in its own interest. None of this suggests that Marx had yet developed a class theory of the state (let alone one articulated with the political economy of capitalism). For, although his contemporary political journalism on such matters as the wood-theft law and the plight of the Moselle peasants alludes constantly to the use of state power to advance particular economic interests,[18] Marx does not integrate these remarks with his view of the Prussian state as a system of political domination to produce an account of the state as an organ of class rule. This is hardly surprising. For, not only was Marx still working within the Hegelian–Feuerbachian approach of his student days in Berlin, for most of this time he was living again in the Rhineland province of Prussia. If his general theoretical view meant that Marx continued to discuss political matters in terms of the opposition between state and civil society rather than class struggle, the fact that the Rhineland was the centre of German industrialism and bourgeois liberalism and was nonetheless oppressed by a strong, feudal state meant that this approach could be applied to contemporary issues without too much difficulty. This should not be taken to imply that Marx was uncritical in his use of the Hegelian framework. For he used the methods of Feuerbachian transformative criticism to reveal the need for the abolition of private property and the abstract state as necessary preconditions for the full realization of democracy and human emancipation. But this commitment was not articulated with a class perspective and remained essentially Jacobin in its overriding concern with popular-democratic struggle.

In contrast Engels underwent a different theoretical development. For, although he was also active in the Young Hegelian movement and became a communist in 1842, it was his stay in Manchester from 1842 to 1844 that was the fundamental formative influence on his understanding of political economy and that enabled him to anticipate the Marxian class theory of the state. Thus, as early as 1843 (while Marx himself was engaged in political journalism and his critique of Hegel), Engels had already written his *Outlines of a Critique of Political Economy* as well as several articles on the social question in England. Moreover, while Marx was busy on his 1844 Paris manuscripts, Engels formulated a preliminary version of the class theory of the state in his articles on the English Constitution and his classic work, *The Condition of the Working Class in England in 1844*. In these studies Engels argues that it is property – specifically the middle class – that rules in England and he describes how 'the bourgeoisie defends its interests with all the power at its disposal by wealth and the might of the state'.[19] Thus, in addition to an examination of the institutional channels through which the political domination of the middle class is secured within the state apparatus, Engels also discusses the class nature of legislation, the common law, the poor law, and philanthrophy.[20] Despite the clarity and vehemence of these analyses, however, Engels does not elaborate them into a general theory of the state. This had to await the collaboration of Marx and Engels in the following years.

The first general formulation of the new approach is found in *The*

German Ideology, written by Marx and Engels in 1845–6 but not published in full until 1932. It was subsequently elaborated in *The Communist Manifesto* and many other political analyses. However, although it is customary to talk about *the* Marxist class theory of the state, these studies do not contain a unitary and coherent analysis. Instead Marx and Engels present a complex array of ideas and arguments unified (if at all) through their common concern with the relations between class struggle and state power within the general framework of historical materialism. Since it is beyond the scope of this short paper to give a full account of these ideas and arguments I shall concentrate on the main themes to be found in the various Marxist analyses of the state.

One of the most prominent themes is the argument that the form of the state is a reflection of the economic base of society and that its interventions are a reflection of the needs of the economy and/or the balance of economic forces. This interpretation of politics in terms of a 'base-superstructure' model is most clearly stated in *The German Ideology, The Poverty of Philosophy*, the *Preface to A Contribution to the Critique of Political Economy*, the third volume of *Capital*, the second part of *Anti-Dühring*, and Engels's letters on historical materialism. In the first of these works, for example, Marx and Engels argue that the state develops with the social division of labour and is the form in which the ruling class asserts its common interests. They also argue that political struggles within the state are merely the illusory forms in which the real struggles of antagonistic classes are fought out.[21] Marx presents similar ideas in *The Poverty of Philosophy* in his observations on the method of political economy.[22] Likewise, in the famous 1859 summary of his general approach, Marx suggests that the relations of production are the real foundation on which rises a legal and political superstructure and to which correspond definite forms of social consciousness.[23] This view is further developed in various parts of *Capital* and is forcefully restated when Marx examines the genesis of capitalist ground-rent. For he argues that '(i)t is always the direct relationship of the owners of the conditions of production to the direct producers – a relation always naturally corresponding to a definite stage in the development of the methods of labour and thereby its social productivity – which reveals the innermost secret, the hidden basis of the entire social structure, and with it the political form of the relation of sovereignty and dependence, in short, the corresponding specific form of the state'.[24] The same theme is taken up by Engels in his critique of Dühring's argument that direct political force is the primary determinant of the economic situation and that the reverse relation is purely secondary in nature.[25] And it is often repeated in Engels's letters on economic determinism.[26]

This theme was described by Marx in his 1859 *Preface* as a guiding thread for his studies and no doubt Engels would acknowledge this too. But it is a thread which is split and frazzled. For it is subject to various twists in their work and is often interwoven with other ideas and themes. At its most extreme this theme could be taken to imply that the state is a pure epiphenomenon of the economic base with no reciprocal effectivity and that there is a perfect correspondence between base and political superstructure. This version is not stated explicitly anywhere in the work of Marx and Engels although certain formulations are capable of such a construction. Instead they tend to argue that different forms of state and state intervention are required by different modes of production and that the nature of state power is determined by the changing needs of the economy and/or by the changing balance of class forces at the economic level. This view is elaborated in relation to various stages in capital accumulation with different forms of state and state intervention required at different stages in its development[27] and it is related to the development of the balance of class forces in struggle as it changes under the impact of the continuing reorganization of the capitalist labour process.[28] In this context Engels also notes that, as a rule, the state cannot oppose the long-run development of the forces of production since this would generally result in the collapse of state power.[29]

That such arguments are not wholly satisfactory is apparent from the qualifications that Marx and Engels themselves often make in their political analyses. But this did not prevent the widespread adoption of simple economism in the Second International nor the development of more complex forms of economic reductionism by the modern 'capital logic' school which attempts to deduce the form, function, and effects of the capitalist state from the nature of the capitalist mode of production considered in isolation.

The theoretical difficulties involved in an exclusive, one-sided emphasis on economic determinism can be stated quite easily. For such a position implies that the economic base is ultimately (if not immediately) self-sufficient and that its spontaneous development is the sole determinant of social evolution. If it is once conceded that the reproduction of the economic base depends on factors outside its control, it follows that its nature and dynamics cannot provide a sufficient explanation for those of society as a whole. This creates insuperable problems for any attempt to reveal a simple correspondence between the relations of production and juridico-political relations and/or between economic classes and political forces. It also implies that political action cannot alter the economic base and/or the nature of class relations until economic factors themselves permit or require such alteration. At most this position allows for temporal deviations in economic development through the introduction of 'leads' or 'lags' between base and superstructure and/or between different levels of the class struggle. It cannot concede more without becoming inconsistent. However, although Marx and Engels emphasized the role of the economic base [*sic*] in social development (especially when engaged in criticism of Hegelian idealism or Dühring's 'force theory'), they do not adopt a monodeterminist position. Instead they are sensitive to the problems involved in economic reductionism and attempt to avoid them through a mixture of qualifications and resort to alternative modes of analysis.

The instrumentalist concept of the state

In this respect it is important to consider the recurrent thesis that the state is an instrument of class rule. For, although it can be assimilated to economic reductionism through the assumption that the economic base determines the form of the state as an instrument and the balance of political forces in the struggle for state power, this thesis can also be developed in a voluntarist direction focusing on the independent role of political action in the transformation of the economic base and the conduct of class struggle. This means that it is important to consider the interpretation which Marx and Engels themselves placed upon the instrumentalist approach.

In its least developed form the instrumentalist approach merely involves the claim that the state is not an independent and sovereign political subject but is an instrument of coercion and administration which can be used for various purposes by whatever interests manage to appropriate it. In this sense Marx had already developed such a view in his 1843 *Critique* and his articles on the wood-theft law and other matters. But it was Engels who first combined this instrumentalist approach with the claim that it was a specific class which controlled the state apparatus and used this control to maintain its economic and political domination. This view is further developed in *The German Ideology*, in which Marx and Engels note that the state is the form in which the individuals of a ruling class assert their common interests;[30] and again in *The Communist Manifesto*, in which they conclude that the executive of the modern state is but a committee for managing the common affairs of the bourgeoisie.[31] Similar remarks occur throughout the subsequent political analyses of Marx and Engels and much of their work is concerned to reveal the various ways in which the modern state is used as an instrument of exploitation of wage-labour by capital.

Moreover, in developing this instrumentalist argument, they also make a fundamental contribution to the analysis of class struggle. For both Marx and Engels are interested in the specific forms and the peculiar dynamics of such struggle at the political level within a social formation as well as in the essential class antagonism at the heart of a pure mode of production. Thus, although they sometimes assert or imply that political class struggle is a simple reflection or, at best, a tendential reflection of the economic conflict between capital and wage-labour, they also frequently refer to complexities introduced through the presence of other classes and social forces and to important discontinuities and dissociations between different levels of class struggle. In this respect it is most instructive to compare the general theory of class struggle offered in the *Communist Manifesto* with the concrete historical analyses presented in the work of Marx and Engels on France, Germany, and England. In the latter we find a wealth of descriptive concepts specific to the political class struggle and its various modalities. For Marx and Engels discuss the relations between class fractions, the role of class alliances, the role of supporting classes such as the smallholding peasantry and the lumpenproletariat, the relations between classes in charge of the state and economically dominant classes, and so forth (cf. Poulantzas, 1973, pp. 229–53). They also examine the role of political parties in the representation of class interests in the struggle for control of the state apparatus and compare it with the effects of Bonapartism and similar forms of executive rule. Thus, at the same time as their analyses of political class struggle reveal the complexities of state power, they also affirm the importance of that struggle in securing control of the state apparatus and shaping its operation. This lends further credence to the instrumentalist approach.

The frequency of such arguments is reflected in subsequent work. For the instrumentalist approach is particularly common in exegeses of the Marxian theory of the state and is widely adopted in more recent Marxist studies. In association with more or less complex forms of economic determinism it can be found in neo-Ricardian analyses and in various studies of 'state monopoly capitalism'. Thus, whilst the neo-Ricardian theorists tend to focus on the instrumentality of the state on behalf of capital in its economic intervention to maintain or restore profits at the expense of wages, 'stamocap' theorists argue that the state and monopolies have 'fused' into a single mechanism which acts on behalf of monopoly capital in the twofold attempt to secure the political and ideological conditions necessary to capital accumulation and to mobilize counter-tendencies to the tendency of the rate of profit to fall. Interpreted in a different manner this view also underlies the reformism of social democratic movements. These tend to see the state apparatus in liberal parliamentary regimes as an independent, neutral instrument which can be used with equal facility and equal effectiveness by all political forces and therefore focus on the pursuit of electoral victory as the necessary precondition of a peaceful and gradual transition to socialism. Instrumentalism is also common among Marxist social and political scientists engaged in theoretical combat with liberal and pluralist positions. A classic in this context is Miliband's study of *The State in Capitalist Society*. But, as the debate between Miliband and Poulantzas indicates, there is far from complete agreement that instrumentalism is the most adequate approach to a Marxist analysis of the state and politics.

Indeed a close examination of the work of Marx and Engels should be sufficient in itself to disclose several problems with such a view. Firstly there is some uncertainty in its formulation. For Marx and Engels generally allude to the simple instrumentality of the state in aphorisms and metaphors rather than more extended and concrete analyses; elsewhere they employ different formulations and contrary arguments. And, if one accepts a simple instrumentalist approach, it is difficult to account for the different forms of the state and to explain why it is necessary to smash the state apparatus rather than seize its control. In general these difficulties are resolved in terms of changes in the economic base and/or in the balance of class forces – solutions which it is difficult to square with the view that the state is an essentially neutral instrument. Moreover, whilst such a view implies that the state apparatus is non-partisan and passive, as early as 1843 Marx had referred to its penetration by competing private interests.[32] Likewise, if the state is a simple instrument of class rule, it is necessary to explain how the dominant mode of production is successfully reproduced when the economically dominant class does not actually occupy the key positions in the state system. This situation is noted by Marx and Engels themselves in relation to the political rule of the landed aristocracy on behalf of capital in nineteenth-century Britain.[33] The same problem is raised when the state apparatus acquires an extensive measure of independence from the dominant class owing to a temporary equilibrium in the class struggle. This situation is alleged to have occurred in the absolutist state, the Second French Empire under Louis Bonaparte, and the German Reich under Bismarck.[34] Indeed, whereas the simple instrumentalist thesis would seem to suggest that the dominant class is generally in immediate control of the state apparatus, it is evident from the many political studies of Marx and Engels that the bourgeoisie is rarely in such a position in any capitalist social formation. This suggests the need for a thorough reappraisal of the instrumentalist reading of the Marxian theory of the state and its subsequent development in the field of Marxist political theory and practice.

In this context we should consider the argument that the state is the factor of cohesion in the social formation. This perspective is closely identified nowadays with the anti-instrumentalist Poulantzas but it is also evident in the classic texts. Thus Marx and Engels argue in *The German Ideology* that an institutionally separate state emerges before the development of class antagonism to manage the common affairs of the members of gentile society. Such an institution is socially necessary because of the mutual interdependence of the individuals in any society with a complex division of social labour.[35] It should be noted that, although this argument is continuous with the Hegelian framework of 'state-civil society' and 'public-private', it is also articulated with concepts relating to class analysis. This is apparent from the subsequent argument that the public power of gentile society is overdetermined in its operation by the emergence of class conflict rooted in an antagonistic mode of production. Thereafter the socially necessary institution becomes a class institution as well and must be sensitive to the complex relations between the common interest and class interests. In this respect Marx and Engels suggest that the conquest of state power presupposes the successful representation of a class interest as the general interest.[36] These ideas are taken up in subsequent analyses by both men but are not stated again with the same clarity and simplicity until Engels presented his general observations on the origins of the state. Thus Marx refers to the English factory acts as essential not only for the working class but also for capital; and Engels discusses the housing question in Germany in similar terms.[37] Likewise Marx notes in *The Eighteenth Brumaire* that the political need to restore social order in France as a precondition of the continued social power of the bourgeoisie induced it to abandon its control over the state apparatus through parliament in favour of a strong executive dominated by Louis Bonaparte.[38] And, of course, in his general treatise on *The Origins of the Family, Private Property, and the State*, Engels argues that the state is necessary to moderate the conflicts between antagonistic classes and keep them within the bounds of social order. This is a complex functional requirement. For, whilst the state must appear to stand above society and keep class antagonisms in check, it is normally the state of the most powerful, economically ruling class, As a rule its class function predominates over its socially necessary function, but exceptional periods occur when the warring classes are so nearly equal in force that the state apparatus, as apparent mediator, acquires for the moment a certain independence from the immediate (or, indeed, indirect) control of these classes.[39] The effects of such an independent state power on social cohesion and capital accumulation need to be examined case by case.

This approach lends itself to various lines of development. Thus Bukharin attempted to develop a scientific analysis of the state in his work on *Historical Materialism*. He treats society as a system of unstable equilibrium inside which the state functions as a 'regulator'.[40] Gramsci is also concerned with the problem of cohesion – albeit from a far less mechanistic position. For Gramsci is especially interested in the ideological practices with which the dominant fraction or class maintains its hegemony through the articulation of popular aspirations and common interests with its own class interests, so that the dominated classes and groups in society consent to their subordination and exploitation.[41] And Poulantzas pursues this line of analysis in his studies of the capitalist state. Indeed, whilst others tend to treat cohesion as a contingent effect of state power, Poulantzas actually defines the state in terms of its necessary and objective function in the maintenance of social cohesion[42] and thus includes all those political and ideological institutions and organizations which contribute to this function within the boundaries of the state. This definition is coupled with an essentialist account of capitalism to produce the conclusion that the state in a capitalist society must, in the long run, reproduce the social conditions necessary for continued capital accumulation and bourgeois hegemony.[43] Lastly it could perhaps be argued that this approach is coupled with economic reductionism in the work of the 'capital logic' school. For this rejects the argument that the state is an instrument of class rule and focuses instead on the vital role of the state in the reproduction of the various social conditions necessary for accumulation in a situation where capital in general exists only in the form of particular, competing capitals.[44]

This approach not only involves serious theoretical difficulties when it is developed in a one-sided manner but it can also produce odd results even in less extreme formulations. Thus, although Poulantzas adopts a functionalist and essentialist definition of the state which refers to its role in the maintenance of social cohesion, he presents several case studies which show that cohesion is a contingent rather than automatic effect of state power. Likewise, although he includes all those apparatuses which contribute to cohesion within the state, his own studies reveal that there are significant differences between liberal and fascist regimes in the articulation of repressive and ideological institutions and organizations.[45] But these differences are difficult to square with his all-inclusive definition of the state.

These inconsistencies in the work of Poulantzas seem less significant, however, when compared with the one-sided arguments developed in other theoretical and political analyses. For, unless one insists with Marx and Engels on the complex and contingent articulation of the socially necessary and the class functions of the state, concern with the role of the state in maintaining social cohesion can easily lead to the conclusion that it can 'reconcile' class conflict by acting as a neutral mediator. But, as Lenin argues forcefully in his monograph on *The State and Revolution*, the state could neither have arisen nor maintained itself had it been possible to reconcile classes. Thus, in opposition to the bourgeois and petty bourgeois politicians who equate social cohesion with class reconciliation, Lenin stresses that 'order' involves the oppression of one class by another and the systematic denial of means and methods of struggle to the oppressed class.[46] And, although Lenin tends to emphasize the repressive side of state power, one can give due weight to the role of ideology and social welfare in the maintenance of cohesion without abandoning his general conclusion that the state is an organ of class domination. But to move from the recognition of the role of 'egemonia' (hegemony) as well as 'dominio' (coercion) in the reproduction of class rule to the argument that the state is neutral and able to reconcile antagonistic classes is clearly to abandon the basic premisses of Marxian political economy and to draw diametrically opposed political conclusions.

Finally it is necessary to consider the presupposition of all the themes and arguments outlined in the present section. For we have not yet established the Marxian definition of the state and examined its implications for political analysis. Indeed, although the point is often overlooked in exegeses of Marxian political theory, the themes and arguments considered above presuppose a definition of the state rather than provide it. Thus the assertion that the state is an epiphenomenon (simple or complex) of an economic base is a theoretical proposition; the claim that the state is an instrument of class rule is best interpreted metaphorically rather than literally; and the view that the state is a factor of cohesion performing socially necessary as well as class functions is an empirical generalization. In short these approaches might usefully be interpreted as adjectival rather than substantive, as predicates rather than subjects, as propositional rather than definitional. This is not to downgrade these approaches but to insist that we reconsider their theoretical status within the Marxian system. In turn this means that we must examine how Marx and Engels defined the state itself.

Marxian definitions of the state

The institutional separation of state and civil society was taken for granted by Marx and Engels in their earliest writings and they did not concern themselves with its genesis until *The German Ideology*. In this work they still take the form of this separate entity for granted and merely allude to its control of military force and its connections with the legal system. In general Marx and Engels view the state as a 'public power' that develops at a certain stage in the social division of labour (usually identified with the emergence of private property and/or modes of production based on the exploitation of one class by another), and which involves the emergence of a distinct system of government separated from the immediate control of the people and/or dominated classes. They generally refer to its control of means of coercion and often employ ostensive definitions which offer a more or less complete list of the institutions that comprise the state.

Thus, in his celebrated study of *The Eighteenth Brumaire of Louis Bonaparte*, Marx refers to the French state as '(t)his executive power, with its enormous bureaucratic and military organization'[47] and proceeds to discuss its forms of representation. Likewise, in his address on *The Civil War in France*, he identifies the same state as the 'centralised state power, with its ubiquitous organs of standing army, police, bureaucracy, clergy, and judicature'.[48] And, in the *Critique of the Gotha Programme*, Marx refers to the Prussian state as 'a state which is nothing but a police-guarded military despotism, embellished with parliamentary forms, alloyed with a feudal admixture, already influenced by the bourgeoisie and bureaucratically carpentered'.[49] Several similar ostensive definitions are offered by Engels in his various studies of England, Germany, and other countries. In addition, in his general treatise on the origins of the state, Engels identifies its defining attributes as organization on a territorial basis, specialized coercive apparatus or force, taxation, administrative staff and, as a rule, political rights graded on a property basis.[50] But it is the less well-formulated definitions that provide the framework within which Marx and Engels develop their arguments about the concentration and centralization of power in the modern military-bureaucratic state and their analyses of the changing balance of political forces in various forms of state in nineteenth-century Europe.

There have been few attempts to develop a Marxist theory of the state based on a narrow institutional definition similar to those of orthodox social and political science. Such an approach has obvious theoretical difficulties for historical materialism since it tends to treat the state as a 'thing' in isolation from other institutions and/or as a separate instance engaged in external relations with other structures. Accordingly the 'relative autonomy' of the state becomes total and the complex internal relations between the different levels of a social formation dominated by a determinate mode of production are also ignored. But, although a narrow institutional approach is usually eschewed in Marxist analyses of the state, many studies adopt an institutional definition in association with an instrumentalist approach in the mistaken belief that this is sufficient to establish the class nature of the state. This is particularly clear in the oft-denigrated but widely-read analysis in Miliband's *The State in Capitalist Society*. Yet even this approach is preferable in certain respects to the *a priorism* of other studies which attribute an essentially capitalist character to the state in capitalist societies.

The latter approach is evident in the economic reductionism of the 'capital logic' school and its analysis of the state as an 'ideal collective capitalist'. It is also evident in the recent debate on the nature of the dictatorship of the proletariat and its implications for political strategy in the workers' movement. Thus, in opposition to the sort of instrumentalism that often underlies the rejection of the dictatorship of the proletariat, Balibar argues that state power is always the political power of a single class, which holds it in an absolute way, does not share it with any other class, and does not divide it up among its own fractions. He also argues that the state power of the ruling class is embodied in the development and operation of the state apparatus which therefore has an absolute and unequivocal class character and cannot be used in neutral fashion.[51] Unfortunately, although this sort of approach may be most valuable in polemical discourse about party strategy, it is most inappropriate to analyses of the complex and contingent articulation of different apparatuses or the effects of state power on the reproduction of bourgeois domination and capital accumulation. In this respect it would be preferable to adopt an institutional approach in combination with a firm grasp of Marxist political economy and an historical appreciation of the nature of class and popular-democratic struggles.

It is significant that Marx and Engels do not offer a conclusive, abstract definition of the state similar to those presented for value, commodity, organic composition, etc., in *Capital*. For, whilst Marx is concerned with the analysis of a pure mode of production in the latter work, it is concrete social formations with which he and Engels are concerned in their various political studies. This has fundamental implications for their analysis of the state in capitalist societies. For, as Marx himself argues in his 1857 *Introduction* to the method and concepts of political economy, 'real-concrete' phenomena cannot be grasped in themselves but must be reconstituted in thought as the 'complex synthesis of multiple determinations'.[52] This implies that the state is both the point of departure and the point of arrival in political analysis since it can only be comprehended after a complex process of theoretical analysis and synthesis. It means that one cannot take the state as an unproblematic empirical given nor reduce it to one of its multiple determinations. Thus, if the narrow institutional approach and the view of the state as a unitary subject share the assumption that the state is a given, economic and class reductionism both take a one-sided approach and define it in relation only to the mode of production or the class struggle. This does not mean that it is illegitimate to focus on particular determinations of the state and state power; nor that it is illegitimate to focus on specific effects of the state and state power on other elements of the social formation or a pure mode of production; but it docs mean that such abstract and restricted forms of analysis are not equivalent to a concrete analysis of specific forms of state or state power in determinate conjunctures.

This is emphasized by Marx in his *Critique of the Gotha Programme* of the German Social Democratic Party. For he argues that, whilst one can generalize about 'present society' across national boundaries, it is impossible to do so about the 'present state'. Thus, whereas capitalism could be found in all 'civilized countries' and varies only in its degree of development, the form of state changes with each country's border and differs between the Prusso–German empire and Switzerland, between England and the United States. However, although Marx concludes that '"*(t)he* present-day state" is, therefore, a fiction', he also argues that modern states share certain essential characteristics. This follows from the fact that, despite their motley diversity of form, states in the civilized countries all stand on the ground of modern bourgeois society. This means that one can talk of 'present states' in contrast to the future when their present root, bourgeois society, will have died off.[53] But it is still necessary to examine each state in its own terms rather than treat all capitalist states as identical because of their common foundation. Thus Marx points out that the failure of the SPD to grasp the fictitious character of 'the present state' leads to a 'riotous misconception' of the Prusso-German empire to which the Social Democrats addressed their demands. In turn this means that their political programme and strategy are dishonest and unworkable.[54] Thus both the 1857 *Introduction* and the 1875 *Critique* suggest that it is incorrect to adopt an essentialist approach to the state and that one must always engage in a complex process of analysis and synthesis in order to comprehend 'present states' and change them.

Continuity and discontinuity in the class theory of the state

We have examined in broad terms the various themes and arguments of
the class theory of the state adopted by Marx and Engels. But our
account still leaves certain questions unanswered. We have suggested
that these themes remain unchanged (except in their articulation with
each other) from *The German Ideology* to the final texts on the state.
Yet we also argued that it was unreasonable to expect the young Marx
to have developed a mature Marxist political theory in his critical
remarks on Hegel and Bauer since he had not yet developed the central
concepts of his mature political economy. Does this imply that there
should be some discontinuity in the development of the class theory?
Conversely, in his analysis of *The Civil War in France*, Marx repeats
the demand for the abolition of the abstract state and the creation of real
democracy. Does this imply that Marx has returned to the themes and
arguments of his Hegelian–Jacobin youth? In short are there major
elements of continuity and/or discontinuity that our rapid overview of
Marxian political theory has distorted or ignored?

It must first be emphasized that the Marxian analysis of state power
was throughout this period basically 'class-theoretical' rather than
'capital-theoretical' in orientation. For Marx and Engels were generally
concerned with political class struggle focused on control of the state
apparatus and its use in the repression of the dominated classes. They
were less often concerned with the integration of the state into the circuit
of capital or the effects of state power on the reproduction of capital.
Marx discusses such topics in detail only in *Capital* and even then
confines the analysis to primitive accumulation, social legislation, and
banking. Likewise, in his analysis of *The Role of Force in History*,
Engels discusses the role of the Prussian state under Bismarck in the
creation of a national market and certain other conditions necessary to
accumulation in Germany.[55] He also notes in *Anti-Dühring* that 'the
modern state . . . is only the organization that bourgeois society takes
on in order to support the general external conditions of the capitalist
mode of production against the encroachments as well of the workers as
of individual capitalists'.[56] It could thus be said that Engels anticipated
the work of the 'capital logic' school on the state as an 'ideal collective
capitalist'. But neither he nor Marx elaborate these insights into a
coherent, general theoretical account of the capitalist state premised on

the nature and dynamics of the capitalist mode of production. And, although it is true that Marx had intended to write on the state in *Das Kapital*, this does not alter the overall lack of such an account elsewhere in their work on political economy. It is for this reason that there may well be more continuity in the Marxian analysis of the state than Marx and Engels themselves may have intended or wished.

In this connection it should also be noted that Marx and Engels do animadvert on the forms of state and law that correspond in various ways to the dominance of the capitalist mode of production. Thus both men discuss the emergence of Roman law and the juristic world outlook with the growth of capitalism and demonstrate how legal equality in the sphere of circulation and exchange underwrites the domination of capital over wage-labour in the sphere of production.[57] And both argue that the development of capitalism permits and/or requires changes in the state apparatus. In particular they refer to the centralization of power in the modern state and the correspondence between capitalism and the parliamentary republican regime.[58] But these arguments are part of the 'base-superstructure' tradition and are not elaborated into an account of the various forms of the capitalist-state. Indeed most of these political tendencies in the modern-state are related not only to the economic base but also to the changing balance of political forces in different countries and conjunctures.

More significant for the overall development of the materialist approach is the analysis of the Paris Commune presented by Marx in his address on *The Civil War in France*. For this text represents a major advance in the Marxian analysis of the state and revolution. In all three drafts of this study Marx emphasizes that, whilst the ruling classes and their different rival fractions can simply lay hold of the existing state apparatus and wield it as a ready-made agency for their own political purposes, it is essential for the working class to smash its repressive machinery and reorganize the way in which its socially necessary functions are performed.[59] The centralized state power of the modern state is said to be the organ of bourgeois domination in France even though it was no longer directly controlled by bourgeois deputies in parliament.[60] In most political upheavals in nineteenth-century France one had seen merely the dwarfish struggle between parliamentary and executive forms of bourgeois class domination. But the Communards were not in revolt against this or that – legitimist, constitutional, republican, or imperialist – form of state power; their revolution was aimed against the state itself so that the people could resume control of its own social life.[61] This is a revolution that can only be carried out by the proletariat since only they have the incentive and power to do away with all classes and all forms of class rule. Indeed, whereas the state apparatus is the organized general organ of political class domination, the Commune is the political form and means of the social emancipation of labour. For the political instrument of working-class enslavement cannot also function as the political instrument of their self-liberation.[62] This requires a revolutionary new form of political organisation which ensures that the people control its own social life through direct and continuous involvement in all facets of government.

Now, although this crucial text is replete with instrumentalist metaphors, its basic thrust is strongly anti-instrumentalist. Indeed Marx implies that the state is a system of political domination whose effectiveness is to be found in its institutional structure as much as the social categories, fractions, or classes that control it. In turn this implies that different forms of state have different effects on the balance of class forces and the course and outcome of political struggles. Thus the analysis of the inherent bias of the system of political representation and state intervention is logically prior to an examination of the social forces that manage to wield state power.

This fundamental insight is emphasized in Lenin's remark in *The State and Revolution* that the bourgeois democratic republic is the best possible political shell for capital and that, once capital has gained possession of this shell, it establishes its power so securely that no change of persons, institutions, or parties can shake it.[63] And it is taken up in the recent German debate with its stress on the separation of the modern bourgeois state from capitalist production as well as on the institutionalization of formal political equality in the bourgeois democratic republic (cf. Holloway and Picciotto, eds, 1977, *passim*).

Unfortunately Marx himself does not develop this new approach in other political studies nor does Engels do more than repeat the arguments in his subsequent work. But it should be clear that, although certain of the ideas first presented in the 1843 *Critique* and 1844 *Introduction* are reproduced in this analysis of the Paris Commune, they have been radically transformed through their articulation with the concepts and principles of Marxian political economy. For the 'abstract state' is now seen as an organ of class domination rather than an expression of the political self-estrangement of private individuals; the 'universal class' is no longer seen as a poverty-stricken mass precipitated through the acute social disintegration of modern society and is now recognized as a wage-labouring class economically exploited through determinate relations of production by capital; and 'real democracy' is no longer premissed on the re-integration of the schizoid 'public' and 'private' lives of modern man but on the class dictatorship of the proletariat in alliance with the urban petty bourgeoisie and the rural peasantry. In short, far from marking a simple return to the radical-liberal groundplan of his political youth, *The Civil War in France* sets the keystone in the arch of Marxian revolutionary theory.

Concluding remarks

We have now examined the youthful philosophical reflections of Marx, the adumbration of a class theory of the state by Engels, its subsequent development by both men, and the final (albeit unfinished) approach implied in their comments on the Paris Commune. But we have not attempted to establish *the* Marxian theory of the state. Indeed an attempt of this kind has been deliberately and studiously avoided throughout. In part this stems from our belief that Marx and Engels adopted different approaches and arguments according to the problems with which they were concerned and did not attempt any systematization of their various forms of analysis. But it also stems from our belief that it is impossible to establish a unitary and coherent theory of the state in general on the basis of the methods and principles of the Marxian critique of political economy.

It is true that Engels wrote a general treatise on the state but its exact theoretical status should be established before we conclude that a general theory of the state is possible. For Engels presents an historical account of three different paths of state formation (in Greece, Rome, and Germany) rather than a single theory of the orgins of the state in general. And he then proceeds to discuss only the most abstract determinations of the state and state power rather than to provide a complete account. This coincides with the arguments propounded by Marx in his 1857 *Introduction* concerning the method of political economy. For he insists that production in general does not exist in the real world but can still be a valid object of analysis in so far as it brings out and fixes the common element in all production and thus saves repetition; but, since production is always production at a definite stage of social development, it is always necessary to analyse production in each epoch as a complex synthesis of general and specific elements. In the same way it can be argued that the state in general is also a rational abstraction but can still be useful in theoretical work to the extent that it brings out the common elements and foundation of all states. Indeed, as Marx himself points out in his 1875 *Critique*, 'the present state' is a valid abstraction based on the essential characteristics of the motley diversity of all bourgeois states. But such conceptions must always be complemented and combined with many other determinations in order to produce an adequate account of concrete forms of state and state power. Thus, although Engels provides certain crucial elements in a Marxist account of the state, his work does not (and cannot) amount to a definitive and exhaustive theory of the state. Only through the synthesis of many different determinations can one move from the abstract to the concrete, and this involves the articulation of different principles of explanation and different modes of analysis. For to attempt to produce a theoretical account of a specific state in a determinate conjuncture on the basis of a single causal principle is to engage in the most extreme form of reductionism or essentialism. In short, whilst a theoretical account of specific states is possible, no single theory of the state can be constructed without rejecting the premises of historical materialism.

This conclusion can be illustrated through the work of Marx and Engels themselves. Most of their political writings were produced to describe specific political events and to situate them in a specific historical context; and/or to provide a theoretical basis for the identification of political class interests and an appropriate mode of intervention in the class struggle. They draw on several different principles of explanation and combine different themes and approaches. They offer a series of acute generalizations and present a number of valuable practical concepts for conjunctural analysis. They focus on the organization of the state apparatus as well as the appropriation and exercise of state power. But they do not offer a systematic and coherent theory of the state based on any one given causal principle or major theme. It is the exegetists who have blocked further advance in the Marxist analysis of the state and state power through their desire to present a simple theory of this kind. This is particularly evident in the facile way in which many subsequent Marxists have seized upon the instrumentalist metaphor to exposit *the* Marxian theory of the state or, alternatively, reduced the state to a more or less complex epiphenomenon of an economic base. Nor is this criticism just a sign of academicism or theoreticism. For, as Marx himself argues in the 1875 *Critique*, errors of analysis in the present state are linked to errors in political practice.

It follows that Marxists today cannot ignore the crucial problems of state power in the formulation of political strategy and tactics in different circumstances. Whilst it is important to recognize the complexities of the current situation and adapt political practice to the changing forms of the state and the changing balance of political forces, it is nonetheless necessary to remember the most abstract determinations of the 'present state' in Marxist analysis. For Marx insisted that, regardless of the specific forms of the modern state, it stood on the ground of capitalist relations of production and had a vital role to play in the process of capital accumulation. This view implies that the abolition of capitalism entails the transformation of the modern state and its characteristic forms of representation and intervention. Furthermore, as Marx argued philosophically in his youth, and in terms of the critique of political economy in his mature political writings, it is not just the capitalist form of state which must be abolished in the transition from capitalism to communism. For it is the historic mission of the communist movement to abolish the state itself – to overcome the separation of state and civil society and to destroy the state as a system of political domination as well as an instrument of class exploitation. In the short term this implies a commitment to popular-democratic struggle as well as class struggle in capitalist societies. In the long term it means that the dictatorship of the proletariat must be a vehicle for the eventual withering away of the state as well as for the creation of communist relations of production. Indeed it is only through the complex articulation of the popular-democratic struggle and the class struggle in appropriate forms of mass organization that it will prove possible to realize the abolition of the abstract state and class exploitation. For, whereas the popular-democratic struggle can be realized only through the creation of the social conditions necessary to popular self-government, the class struggle must be articulated with the values and aspirations of the people if the working class is to isolate and defeat the ruling class. It is in the development of the appropriate forms of struggle that the key to the fulfilment of Marx's revolutionary vision will be discovered.[64]

NOTES

(For Bibliography see below)

1. Colletti, 1975, pp. 45–8.
2. Blackburn, 1976, *passim*.
3. Marx and Engels, *Collected Works*, vol. 3, pp. 3–40 and especially 38–40.
4. Ibid., pp. 20–129.
5. Ibid., pp. 16–17 and 32.
6. Ibid., pp. 45–6.
7. Ibid.
8. Ibid., pp. 98–9 and 108.
9. Ibid., pp. 46 and *passim*.
10. Ibid., pp. 72–3 and 79–81.
11. Ibid., pp. 90–1.
12. Ibid., pp. 122–3.
13. Ibid., pp. 153 and 164.
14. Ibid., pp. 167–8.
15. Ibid., pp. 185–7.
16. Ibid., p. 187.
17. See especially ibid., pp. 187 and 167–8.
18. Marx and Engels, op. cit., vol. 1, pp. 224–63.
19. Op. cit., vol. 4, p. 501.
20. Op. cit., vol. 3, pp. 489–513, and 4, pp. 562–83.
21. Op. cit., vol. 5, pp. 46–7.
22. Op. cit., vol. 6, pp. 161–78.
23. Marx and Engels, *Selected Works*, vol. 1, pp. 503–4.
24. Marx, *Capital*, vol. 3, p. 791.
25. Engels, 1954, pp. 217–55.
26. Marx and Engels, *Selected Correspondence*, 1975, pp. 394–6, 397–401, 433–45, and 441–3.
27. Marx, *Grundrisse*, 1973, p. 651.
28. Cf. Marx and Engels, *Collected Works*, vol. 4, pp. 490–6.
29. Engels, 1954, pp. 253–4.
30. Marx and Engels, *Collected Works*, vol. 5, p. 90.
31. Ibid., vol. 6, p. 486.
32. See the *Critique* in Marx and Engels, *Collected Works*, vol. 3, pp. 3–129.
33. Marx and Engels, *On Britain*, 1962, pp. 423–7.
34. See, for example, Marx and Engels, *Collected Works*, vol. 5, p. 90; Marx and Engels, *Selected Works*, vol. 1, p. 436; and Marx and Engels, *Selected Works*, vol. 3, pp. 328–9.
35. Marx and Engels, *Collected Works*, vol. 5, pp. 46–7.
36. Ibid., p. 60.
37. Marx, *Capital*, I, pp. 264–80; Marx and Engels, *Selected Works*, vol. 2, pp. 323–4 and *passim*.
38. Marx and Engels, *Selected Works*, vol. 1, p. 436.
39. Ibid., vol. 3, pp. 326–9.

40. Bukharin, 1969, pp. 150–4.
41. Gramsci, 1971, *passim*.
42. Poulantzas, 1973, p. 44.
43. Poulantzas, 1976, p. 72.
44. See, for example, Altvater, 1973, *passim*.
45. Poulantzas, 1974, *passim*.
46. Lenin, *Selected Works*, vol. 2, 1963, pp. 290–1.
47. Marx and Engels, *Selected Works*, vol. 1, p. 477.
48. Ibid., vol. 2, p. 217.
49. Ibid., vol. 3, p. 27.
50. Op. cit., pp. 327–8.
51. Balibar, 1977, pp. 64–77.
52. Marx, *Grundrisse*, 1973, p. 101.
53. Marx and Engels, *Selected Works*, vol. 3, p. 26.
54. Ibid., pp. 25 and 27.
55. Ibid., pp. 378–81 and 398–400.
56. Engels, 1954, p. 386.
57. Marx, *Capital*, vol. 1, 1970, pp. 172 and 547; Marx and Engels, *Selected Correspondence*, pp. 355 and 399.
58. See, for example, Marx and Engels, *Collected Works*, vol. 6, p. 486; and Marx and Engels, *Selected Works*, vol. 2, pp. 217–18.
59. Ibid.; and Marx, '*Draft*', 1973, pp. 247–9.
60. Marx and Engels, *Selected Works*, vol. 2, pp. 217–18.
61. Marx, '*Draft*', 1973, p. 249.
62. Marx, '*Draft*', 1973, p. 250.
63. Lenin, *Selected Works*, vol. 2, p. 296.
64. Marx and Engels, *Collected Works*, vol. 3, pp. 185–7.

BIBLIOGRAPHY

Wherever possible reference is made to the *Marx/Engels Collected Works* (London, 1975–).

Altvater, E., 'Notes on Some Problems of State Interventionism', *Kapitalistate*, 1, 1973, pp. 96–108, and 2, 1973, pp. 76–83.

Avinieri, S., *Karl Marx: Social and Political Thought* (London, 1968).

Balibar, E., *The Dictatorship of the Proletariat* (London, 1977).

Blackburn, R., 'Marxism: Theory of Proletarian Revolution', *New Left Review*, 97, May–June 1976, pp. 3–35.

Bukharin, N., *Historical Materialism* (Ann Arbor, 1969).

Colletti, L. (ed.), 'Introduction', *Karl Marx: Early Writings* (Harmondsworth, 1975).

Engels, F., 'The Condition of England: the English Constitution', in Marx and Engels, *Collected Works*, vol. 3 (London, 1975), pp. 489–513.

Engels, F., *The Condition of the Working Class in England in 1844*, in Marx and Engels, *Collected Works*, vol. 4 (London, 1975), pp. 295–590, 489–513.

Engels, F., *The Housing Question*, in Marx and Engels, *Selected Works*, vol. 2 (Moscow, 1969), pp. 295–375.

Engels, F., *Anti-Dühring* (Moscow, 1954).

Engels, F., *The Origins of the Family, Private Property, and the State*, in Marx and Engels, *Selected Works*, vol. 3 (Moscow, 1969), pp. 204–334.

Engels, F., *The Role of Force in History*, in Marx and Engels, *Selected Works*, vol. 3 (Moscow, 1969), pp. 377–428.

Holloway, J., and Picciotto, S. (eds), *Capital and the State: A German Debate* (London, 1978).

Lenin, V. I., *State and Revolution*, in V. I. Lenin, *Selected Works*, vol. 2 (Moscow, 1963), pp. 283–376.

Marx, K., *Contribution to the Critique of Hegel's Philosophy of Law*, in Marx and Engels, *Collected Works*, vol. 3 (London, 1975), pp. 3–129.

Marx, K., *On the Jewish Question*, in Marx and Engels, *Collected Works*, vol. 3 (London, 1975), pp. 146–74.

Marx, K., *Contribution to the Critique of Hegel's Philosophy of Law: Introduction*, in Marx and Engels, *Collected Works*, vol. 3 (London, 1975), pp. 175–87.

Marx, K., *The Economic and Philosophical Manuscripts*, in Marx and Engels, *Collected Works*, vol. 3 (London, 1975), pp. 229–346.

Marx, K., *The Poverty of Philosophy*, in Marx and Engels, *Collected Works*, vol. 4 (London, 1976), pp. 105–211.

Marx, K., *The Class Struggles in France 1848–1850*, in Marx and Engels, *Selected Works*, vol. 2 (Moscow, 1969), pp. 205–99.

Marx, K., *The Eighteenth Brumaire of Louis Bonaparte*, in Marx and Engels, *Selected Works*, vol. 2 (Moscow, 1969), pp. 398–477.

Marx, K., *Introduction to a Contribution to the Critique of Political Economy* in *Grundrisse*, ed. M. Nicolaus (Harmondsworth, 1973), pp. 81–114.

Marx, K., *Grundrisse: Foundations of the Critique of Political Economy (Rough draft)*, ed. M. Nicolaus (Harmondsworth, 1973), pp. 115–893.

Marx, K., *Preface to a Contribution to the Critique of Political Economy* in Marx and Engels, *Selected Works*, vol. 1 (Moscow, 1969), pp. 502–6.

Marx, K., *Capital*, in three volumes (Moscow, 1970).

Marx, K., *The Civil War in France*, in Marx and Engels, *Selected Works*, vol. 2, (Moscow, 1969), pp. 178–243.

Marx, K., 'The First Draft of the Civil War in France (Extract)', in *Marx: The First International and After*, ed. D. Fernbach (Harmondsworth, 1973), pp. 236–68.

Marx, K., 'Marginal Notes to the Programme of the German Workers' Party', in Marx and Engels, *Selected Works*, vol. 3 (Moscow, 1969), pp. 13–30.

Marx, K., and Engels, F., *Selected Works in Three Volumes*, Moscow, 1969.

Marx, K. and Engels, F., *The German Ideology*, in *Collected Works*, vol. 4 (London, 1976), pp. 20–539.

Marx, K., and Engels, F., *The Manifesto of the Communist Party*, in *Collected Works*, vol. 6 (London, 1976), pp. 477–519.

Marx, K., and Engels, F., *On Britain* (Moscow, 1962).

Marx, K., and Engels, F., *Selected Correspondence* (Moscow, 3rd edn, 1975).

Miliband, R., *The State in Capitalist Society* (London, 1968).

Poulantzas, N. *Political Power and Social Classes* (London, 1973).

Poulantzas, N., *Fascism and Dictatorship* (London, 1974).

Poulantzas, N., 'The Capitalist State', *New Left Review*, 95, Jan.–Feb., 1976, pp. 63–83.

IAN CONNELL

MONOPOLY CAPITALISM AND THE MEDIA
Definitions and Struggles

The media and relative autonomy

It is a commonplace in many radical critiques of current media practices to assert that their products are ideological. By this it is usually meant that films, television programmes and all the other products of the 'consciousness industry' provide 'biased' or 'false' accounts of an independent 'reality'. These accounts are false and distort reality – so the argument runs – because of the direct and pervasive influence on them of dominant or ruling class ideas. These ideas are, in turn, conceived as the coherent articulation of this entire class's economic and political interests. In short, the media are said to be the means by which the interests of this class are amplified and generalized across the entire social formation. The media function unambiguously, so it would seem, as the ideological executive of the ruling class.

The primary aim of this paper is to offer a more adequate account of the media and their practices than the one which is proposed by the above critique, which is open to attack on several accounts. All too often, for example, attempts to determine the ideological character and effects of the media have argued directly from an analysis of the economic forms of organization of the media. One consequence of doing this is to make it appear as if the ideological effects constructed by media messages were the inevitable outcome of the economic practices of the media industries. This is a tendency which can be seen in Murdock and Golding's attempts to construct a map of 'the political economy of mass communications' (in their article in *Socialist Register 1973* and in their more recent essay, 'Capitalism, Communication and Class Relations' (1977)).*

* See p. 97 for Bibliography.

Before considering the shortcomings and errors of this tendency, it should be said that Murdock and Golding have made considerable and positive contributions to our understanding of both media practices and their effects. They have recognized the need to get beyond the simple, moral condemnations of the forms of ownership of the media, still fashionable with liberal critics. They have also suggested the inadequacies of those studies which have focused on 'anecdotal accounts of isolated incidents of suppression or manipulation', pointing out that they rarely provide insights into the *routine* and *typical* character of media practices. Furthermore, they have recognized that tensions can and do exist between entrepreneurial strategies governed by the 'logic of profitability' on the one hand, and what we might think of as the communicative strategies and logics of those directly engaged in the production of media products, on the other. They have argued that 'the balance between commodity production and creativity is a precarious one, and one which is ultimately framed and determined by the general economic context within which production takes place' (1974, p. 223). In more general terms, in their latest paper on the subject, it is argued that

> marxism's distinctiveness and promise as a framework for the sociological analysis of culture and communication lies precisely in the fact that it focuses on the *complex connections* between base and superstructure. Once these connections are devalued or left undeveloped, much of marxism's theoretical power evaporates (1977, p. 19)

These remarks would suggest that the authors are working with a model of the social formation, and of the media's place and role within it, that avoids the simplicities and reductions of economic determinism. Indeed, they state at one point in their most recent paper that 'we have said that economics are not the sole determinant of media behaviour, and in this sense we are not arguing a thesis of bald economic determinism'. However, these indications that an adequately complex model is being employed – one, that is, which allows for, and provides some account of, the specific properties and effectivities of ideological practices – are belied by the actual analysis. What, in practice, they provide us with is an analysis which one-sidedly concentrates on economic factors and which assumes that it is possible to read off the ideological effects of the media without specific and detailed attention to ideological practices themselves.

Murdock and Golding suggest that, in periods of economic stringency especially, though by no means exclusively, 'the criteria of cost-effectiveness are likely to be decisive with the result that production will be characterised by a systematic rejection of the unpopular and a reversion to formulae with a proven market potential' (1974, p. 224). The cumulative effect of this apparent dominance of 'cost-effectiveness', the tendency to diversify across the spectrum of culture industries, and the tendency to monopoly forms of ownership of the apparatuses of media production is, they argue, 'increasingly to limit the variety of entertainment and leisure options on offer to the majority of people and to standardize content' (ibid., p. 226), and moreover leads to the production of 'a cultural artefact which legitimates the consensus' (ibid., p. 228). In short, they assume a *tight and necessary correspondence* between market forces and decisions on the one hand, and the nature of the media's ideological output on the other.

It is because of this leap that it is necessary to part company with their approach and their conclusions. It cannot be denied that economic factors do have a bearing on media practices. A longstanding problem with the British film industry, for example, with which legislation and economic policies since the 1920s have failed to deal, is the creaming off of profits from the industry. Indeed, much of the legislation has dealt only with distribution and exhibition and in such ways that the problem of the lack of capital investment in domestic production has been exacerbated. Nor is there any doubt that cinema entrepreneurs are motivated to make, and privately appropriate, profits. But having said this, there is no guarantee that if the cinema were 'nationalised' tomorrow, that is, legally owned by the state, there would be a transformation of its output. It would not mean that from then on films would be produced that attempted to define and generalise the interests of the proletariat. The cinema, like television, is regarded by the state as an 'important factor in the education of all classes of the community in the spread of a "national" culture'; to transform these sentiments requires action of a different kind, namely, ideological action.

It is untenable to suggest that the monopolization of particular cultural industries has, in itself, given rise to 'limiting the leisure options open to people'. Murdock and Golding's formulations imply that prior to monopoly forms of ownership, there were more options available. This is tantamount to saying of the film industry that, prior to the late fifties and early sixties (when declining audiences accelerated the tendency to monopolization), because there were a greater number of brand names there was a plurality of choice: in this case the ideological premisses of United Artists' pictures would have to have been wholly different from, say, those of Universal Pictures.

Nor is it tenable to suggest that the phenomenon of standardization – the establishment and routinization of a repertoire of formal devices, the recurrence of a certain set of topics, and the ideological thematization of them in established and familiar ways – is simply the peculiar outcome of a culture industry organized in monopoly or big capital form. The standardization of message forms can be detected in other phases of capitalism, and indeed, even in precapitalist modes of production. It is also the case that certain forms of discourse, routinely employed in these precapitalist modes of production, are currently employed in this moment of the capitalist mode: the commentary, as it is to be found in News and Current Affairs broadcasting and in Documentary Features, performs textual and ideological functions similar to those of the chorus in Greek tragedy. If we propose the tight correspondence between the economic and the cultural that Murdock and Golding do, we have no way of explaining the current use of these cultural traces.

The general point to be made against the kind of approach adopted by Murdock and Golding is that it fails to *identify and to take account of the relatively autonomous level of communicative-ideological determination*. The choice of format, for instance, within a given sector of the media is never made solely with reference to the criteria of cost-effectiveness, but also, and moreover, *in the first instance* with reference to the criteria of *communicative-effectivity*. While cultural entrepreneurs may well place a different weight and emphasis on the latter, they too must take these criteria into account if they are to produce a cultural commodity that will generate profits. From the outset, however, Murdock and Golding have argued that 'the obvious starting point for a political economy of the media is the recognition that the mass media are first and foremost industrial or commercial organizations which produce and distribute commodities' and only then do they add as a nagging afterthought that '*in addition* (my italics) to producing and distributing commodities, however, the mass media also disseminate ideas about economic and political structures' (1974, p. 205–6).

If anything, our starting point is the reverse of theirs. From our alternative perspective, the media are conceived of as principally organizations for the production and distribution of a 'Public' discourse about the controversial events that occur in the social formation at a given moment in time. To summarize, our objections to the perspective elaborated by Murdock and Golding are:

(1) that the communicative and ideological dimensions of message production are cast as secondary or 'additional';
(2) that this is so because for them production and the social relations of message production are conceived of as purely economic, this ignores the fact that the object of media practices is a message, a sign vehicle constituted within the rules of language; it is in this phenomenal form, the form of an audio-visual discourse, that the circulation of the product takes place; and it ignores the fact that the social relations of this specific form of production are *communicative relations*;
(3) because the peculiarities or specificities of media production and its commodities are ignored, certain ideological effects are abstractly imputed; no analysis is provided of how these effects are constructed and realized within the discourse.

For many, not just Murdock and Golding, it appears 'obvious' that the media should produce 'cultural artefacts' that 'legitimate the consensus'. In their most recent essay, Murdock and Golding summarize this position thus:

Given the insistent pressure to maximize audiences and revenues there is not surprisingly a consistent tendency for the commercial media to avoid the unpopular and tendentious and to draw instead on the values and assumptions which are most familiar and most widely legitimated, *which almost inevitably means those which flow authoritatively downwards through the social structure*. Hence, because dissenting and oppositional views do not fit very easily into the prevailing frameworks of imagery and expression, they tend to be excluded (1977, pp. 37–8).

In other words the media only articulate already legitimated values and assumptions and facilitate their 'downward' flow – a 'flow' hardly impeded by resistance.

Murdock and Golding, like some others, have based these conclusions on certain propositions set out by Marx in *The German Ideology*. Particular use is made of Marx's argument that:

The class which has the means of material production at its disposal has control at the same time over the means of mental production, so that thereby, generally speaking, the ideas of those who lack the means of mental production are subject to it (1938, p. 39).

The closeness of Murdock and Golding's position to this is made clear when they argue that

> ... while their position as owners made the capitalist class the dominant economic class, their consequent control over the production and distribution of material goods and symbol systems provided the means through which this domination was maintained (1977, p. 28).

In their formulation, however, the qualifications present in Marx's are removed. Control of the production and distribution of 'symbol systems' is cast as a consequence of being the dominant class at the economic level, and this symbol system is moreover also presented as being exclusively harnessed to the reproduction of this economic dominance.

There are two major assumptions implicit in both formulations which are open to criticism. The first is the assumption that the dominant economic class is *also* dominant politically and ideologically. Ownership of the means of material production is considered sufficient to guarantee ideological and political domination over subordinate classes. Such an assumption rests, as Althusser and others have pointed out, on the notion that there is a tacit identity between the economic and other levels of a social formation. These other levels – the political and the ideological – become mere epiphenomena of the economic base in a model of social formations which reverses, *but remains essentially the same as*, the Hegelian model. It is worth noting, however, that this model was subjected to criticism and rejected even before Althusser's extremely important critique, by Marx himself, for example, in his analysis of the complexities of the Eighteenth Brumaire of Louis Bonaparte. (For a perceptive account of how the *historical* transformations occurring in France at that moment required an abandonment by Marx of the simple 'base-superstructure' formulations of, for example, *The German Ideology* and *The Communist Manifesto*, see Hall, 1977.) Marx's other model, one which was only fleetingly developed, insisted on the need to grasp the relations and *reciprocal* determinations between 'the economic foundation' and 'the whole immense superstructure' as complex and not simply reflexive, transparent, or unmediated.

The second assumption, which follows from the first, is that the rule of the dominant economic class (the 'entire' bourgeoisie) on the ideological level is not only absolute but requires no ideological labour. For Murdock and Golding and others, 'beliefs about the *inevitability* of a given social order, about the limits of acceptable social practice and values, *are diffused throughout* the social structure' (1977, p. 35). In short, the entire social formation is so thoroughly permeated by the 'world view' of the dominant economic class that it is a wonder to Murdock and Golding that 'oppositional values ever emerge'. For them, ideological oppositions are not regarded as intrinsic to capitalist social formations. It follows from this that they see the media as empty of oppositional values and definitions and, more generally, the ideological level as the site of the abolition of the primary, and indeed, *all* other contradictions. The ruling class not only aspires to, but has apparently succeeded in, exercising a *total* social authority over subordinate classes so that these classes have no option but to live out their relations to production within the terms of reference set down by the dominant class. And the dominant class has accomplished all this immaculately, without engaging in a single ideological labour or struggle.

If the class struggle exists at all, it does so, for accounts such as this, only on the economic level. Ideology merely reflects the state of that economic struggle; it is not itself a site of class struggle, not *the* realm in which people become conscious of conflicts and fight them out. Rather, it is made to appear as if it were in ideology that economic struggles between the fundamental classes were 'magically resolved', always, invariably to the profit of the dominant economic class factions. It is an approach which presupposes a 'teeth gritting harmony' (in Althusser's phrase) between the dominant economic classes and their ideological agents in the media; that assumes that these agents' products are closed up around one real and unambiguous class meaning. and that all audiences will always be bound to these media products in a transparent and passive relation – in short, that all audiences will read the messages exactly as the media producers and their class masters intended. Thus, public communication is, or would seem to be, a process without opposition, discontinuities or breaks.

The position advocated against this model begins from a rather different set of premises. As has already been indicated, the first of these is that the media belong first and foremost to the region of ideology. They embody discrete forms of ideological practice which have 'men's (and women's) consciousness' as their raw material.

That consciousness upon which they act and ultimately work to reproduce and generalize is not, however, the exclusive property of that class which can be identified as dominant at the economic level. To argue the opposite not only supposes a simple identity between that class and those ideologues employed in the media, but also suggests that there are already in existence fully formed, coherent class ideologies – ruling class ideologies at any rate – upon which these ideologues can draw. Suppositions like this, as Poulantzas has argued in his critique of 'historicist' conceptions of ideology, are oversimplifications with drastic consequences for political, and indeed, ideological struggle. First, the over-politicization of ideology, in which ideologies are treated 'as if they were political number plates worn by social classes on their backs' makes it impossible to decipher the concrete relation between the dominant ideology and the politically dominant class faction. Poulantzas has suggested that

> in reality, the dominant ideology does not simply reflect the conditions of existence of the dominant class, the 'pure and simple' subject, but rather the concrete political relation between the dominant and dominated classes in a social formation. It is often permeated by elements stemming from the 'way of life' of classes or fractions other than the dominant class or fraction (1975, p. 203).

These observations constitute an important opening in the reformulation of questions about ideology and ideological struggles. Above all, by removing ideology from its construction by a single class subject – the dominant economic class – they raise the possibility of thinking the dominant ideology as a 'complex unity'.

In other words, they suggest that the ruling or dominant ideology is not the ideology of any single class. It is rather a formation which is relatively autonomous of the various sectional ideologies of the dominant economic and political classes. The dominant ideology exists in a relatively autonomous relation to 'class' ideologies for a number of reasons. First, it is, as Poulantzas has suggested, a *composite structure* fashioned out of the sectional ideologies peculiar to politically and economically ruling-class factions and *also* out of those peculiar to certain subordinate class factions. But more than this, the dominant ideology is a composite that *cannot* be reduced to any one of these ideological sub-ensembles: it is not simply the sum of its constituent parts. Rather, it presents its own unity which can be perceived in (a) its 'isolation-effects' and in (b) in its articulation of 'the will to nationhood'.

To put this another way, dominant ideological practices contribute to the practical deconstruction of potential social classes into competitive individuals and pressure groups of one kind and another. They contribute in the sense that this process of decompostion is initiated elsewhere, in the labour process and, especially, in exchange (cf. Clarke, *et al.*, 1977). However, the dominant ideological practices reconstruct these 'free' individuals, not into the unity of a class, but into the unity of the nation: they moderate and mediate the competitive struggles between groups 'in the national interest'.

There is another reason for arguing that this dominant ideology, which *defines the nation and national interests*, is relatively autonomous. This is that there is no such thing as *the* ideology of the ruling class, or even *the* ideology of the working class. Apart from the dominant ideology, there exist only loosely federated sectional ideologies – fragmentary, localized 'sub-cultures'. Ultimately this is so because the fundamental classes do not yet exist and operate as 'classes-for-themselves'. This is not to argue that classes do not exist, but rather, to argue that they do not make their appearance as fully formed homogeneous forces. The *apparent* reality is of competitive groups of labourers, management, consumers and their various 'representative' bodies. It is this *lived* reality which dominant ideological practices adopt and render 'obvious'.

The hegemonic rule or, as Wright Mills put it, 'power justified by the beliefs of the voluntarily obedient' to which dominant, capitalist classes and class factions aspire, depends upon this relative autonomy of the dominant ideology. Incapable of ruling on its own, because of the internal contradictions that factionalize capital, this class must attempt to win and maintain alliances with its own factions, and other 'subaltern' classes. When a class rules by means of such alliances it must be both capable of making real economic and political concessions to its allies and of winning their consent. Wright Mills, again, has pointed out that it is an error to equate power with coercion: this is but one form of power, the ultimate form, and for Wright Mills the contemporary formation (the 'Cold War' period) was far from that last instance situation when this form of power predominated. In addition to coercion, there is also the power to define situations and issues in ways which provide 'the horizon of thought and action within which conflicts are fought out. . . . A hegemonic order prescribes not the specific content of ideas but the limits within which ideas and conflicts move and are resolved' (Clarke, *et al.*, 1976, p. 39).

It would be a mistake to presume the success of hegemonic strategies, to presume that consent is actually secured, or that when it is what we witness is the complete incorporation of subordinate class factions. It has recently been argued that 'hegemony is not universal and given to the continuing rule of a particular (ruling) class. It has to be won, worked for, reproduced, sustained' (Clarke *et al.*, 1975, p. 60). This is so because, as Althusser for one has insisted, there is *Ideological class struggle*:

> The class (or class alliance) in power cannot lay down the law in the ISAs (media, education, the church) as easily as it can in the (repressive) State apparatuses, not only because former ruling classes are able to retain strong positions there for a long time, but also because the *resistance of exploited classes is able to find means and occasions to express itself there*, either by the utilisation of their contradictions, or by conquering combat positions in them in struggle (1971, p. 140).

Hegemonic rule can never be absolute because it is the reproduction of a constantly antagonistic relation. While the ideological labour which is necessary to it may contribute to the achievement of momentary, negotiated settlements, it cannot dissolve the fundamental contradictions. Nor are the ideological practices by which these settlements are attempted without contradiction. There are indeed antagonistic oppositions at this level – between, on the one hand, distinct schools of professional communicators and, on the other, between communicators and the audiences who consume their products. With respect to the latter, there is *no* evidence to suggest that all the social groups that comprise the audience for the media's accounts of a given situation will accept, without qualification, the orientations and positions those accounts offer.

Before demonstrating the nature of these contradictions, let us see how the broader, theoretical issues that have so far been discussed relate to the alternative view of the media, in particular of television, advocated here.

Unlike the standard radical critique, this does not assume that television performs its ideological work on behalf of the ruling classes by being 'biased' in any simple, conspiratorial sense. The coverage of problematic issues and events offered by television programmes does not systematically prefer any one of the sectional ideologies peculiar to these ruling classes. Differences, often of an antagonistic type, can be detected between the accounts given by broadcasters and those given by the primary representatives of ruling class factions. These differences are a consequence of the fundamental editorial imperatives that govern broadcasting. We cannot begin to determine the ideological character of television programmes, or the nature of the relation between broadcasters and politically-ruling and economically-dominant class factions unless we have first specified the effects of these editorial imperatives.

Television programmes are, as their defenders have consistently asserted, habitually and scrupulously impartial and objective in surveilling and in attempting to explain current and controversial issues. The production of a discourse that is routinely impartial and objective is the principal means by which its relative autonomy is secured from particular, sectional definitions. The News and Current Affairs coverage of industrial struggles, for example, does not present a consistently one-sided account. Rather, it will always attempt to provide, as fully and as faithfully as possible, an account of *each* of the *major* sectional interests and definitions that are in play. Hence, in the case of serious industrial struggles, television journalists will make sure that they consult *both* sides of the House of Commons, and representatives of *both* sides of industry. Their relative independence from each of these will also be maintained by presenting themselves as 'our' representatives; they ask their questions on behalf of that seemingly non-aligned 'general public'.

Nevertheless, the fulfillment of this editorial policy does not lead to the production of a discourse that is ideologically inert, as many a professional broadcaster supposes. Television programmes are massively oriented towards only certain kinds of definitions and explanations of problematic situations. The explanations that are adopted and preferred by television programmes are those consistent with 'common sense', 'moderate public opinion', the 'consensus' – in short, those dominant ideas with which 'the-nation-as-a-whole' is assumed to be familiar and to take for granted. Television's contribution to the reproduction of existing social relations of production and of power is located in its continuous re-affirmation that the dominant ideology is shared by the nation. It accomplishes this not *despite* impartiality and objectivity, but *precisely* because they are diligently realized in every programme.

Television, current affairs and the end of consensus

The routine and extensive use of the complex genre of television journalism to provide coverage of the topical and novel, through to the intensely problematic issues of the moment, has been a comparatively recent development in the history of broadcasting. It was not until the introduction of Independent Television in 1955 that News and Current Affairs departments committed above all else to the norms and objectives of 'professional' journalism began to emerge as prominent and powerful broadcasting forces, and only through the decade 1956–66 that their output came to occupy key positions in the schedules of both networks. Only by 1966 did there exist an extensive and, for the first time in the BBC, a centrally coordinated framework of programmes devoted to surveilling and inviting comment on current 'national' issues.

The transformation of the 1956–66 period challenged the supremacy of the longstanding, didactic traditions of the BBC, and involved a whole new breed of 'professional broadcasters', many of them recruited into television for the first time during the 1950s, in often bitter struggles with the editorial executive of the BBC and the commercial managements of the companies affiliated to the then Independent Television Authority (ITA). Sir Hugh Greene, who became Director-General of the BBC in 1959 summed up the mood of this change when he wrote 'the face of broadcasting was fundamentally changed. . . . Broadcasting is no longer a profession for gentlemen; the players have taken over' (Greene, 1969, p. 11).

These new 'players' challenged the existing traditions in order to connect with what had come to be identified as the 'mass' audience. The type of journalism that they fought to introduce during these years had hitherto been confined to the peripheries: it had not been employed on 'headline' or 'hard' news stories. A good example of this style of journalism was to be found in the programme *Special Enquiry*, first transmitted in the autumn of 1952. Many of the techniques it employed were adopted into hard core journalism in the post 1955 years, after the introduction of Independent Television News (ITN).

Special Enquiry closely followed another, American, programme called *See it Now*. According to Norman Swallow who produced *Special Enquiry*, the attractiveness of the American programme was that although the BBC, like CBS, was unable to have any editorial opinion of its own, it could at least have a broad point of view, and it seemed to those of us who were concerned with the birth of *Special Enquiry* that one of the most exciting merits of *See it Now* was the way in which (Ed) Murrow had seemed to place himself *on the side of the audience.* His approach was that of the hardened reporter whose concern was to find out the facts on behalf of the viewer, and to let nothing and nobody stand in his way (Swallow, 1966, p. 73).

This seeming identification with the audience was recreated for *Special Enquiry* by the use of a number of techniques which were then novel to television journalism, but which now constitute standard practices. First the man selected to present the programme was Robert Reid, whose 'slight northern accent added to his earthy, no-nonsense approach'. For Norman Swallow, 'this was clearly no routine spokesman for the Establishment, but a man to be trusted – one of "us" rather than one of "them" ' (Swallow, ibid.).

In his introductions, Reid – this 'extra-ordinary' spokesman for the Establishment – made every effort to connect the given topic to some aspect of what was considered 'ordinary' or 'everyday' experience. An item on the problems of refugees who had fled from 'East' to 'West' Germany, transmitted in July 1953, demonstrates the characteristic ways in which this complicity with audiences was attempted:

> Now this is the beginning of the Bank Holiday weekend, and I should imagine that a lot of you will be setting off tomorrow, abroad on the continent, possibly for the first time in your lives. Well, you'll find it strange and charming, and you'll enjoy it, but at the same time there will be quite a big reservation at the back of your minds. I don't think you'd like to swap all that novelty permanently for that little semi-detached on the outskirts of Bradford, for the bowling club and the mill, all your old friends, the chapel, the local paper and so on. You see these sorts of things are the things which give a man his roots in life – the place he knows, the people he knows. . . .
>
> One evening when you are sitting in one of those little comfortable street cafes, with the missus, just having a drink, secure in the knowledge that you have in your pocket a British passport . . . I want you to imagine that by some monstrous stroke of fate . . . your home, your family, your friends, everything that has meant life to you, have been suddenly cut off from you.
>
> Well, if you can project yourself into a situation of that sort – just for a moment – it will give you some idea of the human problem we're going to tackle tonight . . . (BBC, Programme transcript).

So, the attempted connections proceed (a) by the use of a colloquial linguistic register, (b) by summoning up what seem to the presenter to be familiar and ordinary experiences and setting these against some of the novel experiences of 'affluence', and (c) by locating Reid as one attuned to the familiar, but at the same time one 'in the know' about such exotic things as 'comfortable street cafes'. In other words, Reid acts as a mediator, linking the ordinary world of the viewer to other worlds beyond their immediate ken. This mediating role became routinized during this period and is now diffused throughout the Current Affairs field – until recently Michael Barratt on *Nationwide*, David Dimbleby on *Panorama* and Denis Tuohy on *Tonight*, each of them regarded as figures who personify characteristics which are taken to be typical of the 'target' audience.

Another feature of the transformation was the use in News, especially ITN in the first instance, of the 'vox pop' or 'man-in-the-street' interview. With ITN it was developed as a constituent part of the coverage of 'hard' news stories. For Robin Day, such interviews could be valuable in several ways:

> Their spontaneous comments can sum up widely held opinions in clear, down-to-earth language. At a big moment they can catch the mood of ordinary people – bitter, excited, overjoyed, bewildered. They can show whether any clear or informed public opinion exists on a particular issue (Day, 1961, p. 121).

They were best used when 'the topic is very close to the personal lives of the people questioned (fares, traffic, a local dispute). . .'. Such interviews were definitely not to be used to *establish* 'divisions of opinions', but rather simply reflect those divisions that had already been identified by other, more authoritative sources.

The development of this type of interview, and of the *actuality* film techniques which it required, had a dual function. It served first of all to *ground* and *authenticate* television's coverage of problematic issues. Their use contributed to the construction of 'the living reality' effect which objective journalists sought after. As Cardiff (1975) has said of the contemporary use of this type of interview, 'its function is to give a "thermometer reading" of public feeling on a given issue'. At the same time, it also functions as a *point of identification*, potentially at any rate, for the audience. Cardiff, again, says

> by presenting a thermometer reading of what the 'man-in-the-street' thinks about it all, the medium is in effect offering the listening public a picture of

itself, and inviting the audience to identify with the stylistically established frame of reference (1975, p. 23)

These and other innovations such as the 'probing interview' which was developed to handle 'public representatives', politicians in particular, stemmed from the perceived need on the part of the new journalists to make News and Current Affairs' definitions of situations available, acceptable and interesting to a large 'popular' audience. As in earlier moments, they still attempted to provide accounts which were 'realistic', consistent with the basic editorial imperatives and rationale. But, it was now recognised that this was insufficient to gain the interest of audiences and from this observation arose the attempts to get messages across 'in terms that the ordinary viewer will understand'. Ultimately, these concerns stemmed from the changing composition, and partial decomposition, of the 'national culture'. With the waning hegemony of traditional authority, the ascendancy of parliament and its ritualized oppositions as the new locus of authority, and with the increasing awareness of the absence of a universal and wholehearted involvement in parliamentary procedures on the part of 'ordinary voters (according to political sociologists, the 'apathetic'), the construction of accounts which were thought to command national assent was no longer the smooth task it had once been in the halcyon days of Reithian broadcasting.

The dark side of the liberal ethos which had fired the efforts of the new journalists and had displaced the reverential ethos which had inspired Richard Dimbleby's awed commentaries on regal rituals, was that there were very few areas of life remaining on which it was possible to provide an account with which 'everyone could agree'. The notion that programmes could provide absolute or 'natural' truths was now firmly relegated to the realms of the ideal. The new professionals had to be content with reporting that 'while many people had said this . . . many others had said that', and then inviting the primary protagonists to participate in speculative probing and discussion in an attempt to discover the most plausible account available. Hence, the adoption of the 'hard', 'tough' style of interviewing, the leading exponent of which is still Robin Day, which was legitimized as an attempt 'to get at the facts' on behalf of the public. This adoption of a 'watchdog' role on behalf of ordinary voters also led to the attempted identifications with 'us', and the attempts to articulate the kinds of questions that 'we' would ask of 'our' powerful representatives if 'we' only could.

Between 1966 and today there have been several moments when the complement of journalistic programmes has been selectively overhauled and modified. Some new faces have been introduced to present programmes, though many more have remained 'up front' throughout. However, no major formal innovations have been carried through in these years: experimentation and innovation have been, at best, fragmentary and fleeting, typically resulting in a return to the norm. What has happened has been an overall tendency to revision and retrenchment, intensified in the last decade in the aftermath of the parliamentary critique of broadcasting, which has involved both the leading political parties in only superficially differing ways. This critique hinged on the assumption that the broadcasting authorities, the BBC especially, had become too independent, showing responsibility to neither parliament nor public. This, in turn, was founded on the notion that broadcasting has accelerated, at times wittingly, the current decomposition of parliamentary authority and with it, national values and beliefs. Spokesmen for television have counter-attacked by denying the latter accusation outright, and by arguing that 'the primary duty of broadcasting organizations within a parlimentary democracy' is 'to sustain, and support to the utmost, the democratic system and the rule of law which is the necessary partner of that system' (Cox, 1976, p. 627). At the same time, formal modifications to programmes have been carried out in order that this 'support to the utmost' can be practically demonstrated.

The author of these remarks, Sir Geoffrey Cox, has also remarked that one of the 'intelligible principles' of broadcasting is that it should be carried out 'in the public interest'. But, he has asked, 'how do we define the public interest in a society whose fundamental assumptions are under challenge?'

> The assumptions of what constituted the public interest were easier to make in Britain ten years ago. Faith in Parliamentary democracy and the rule of law, the family, even Christian morality was firm, under challenge only from dogmatic groups of little power. But now, instead of such beliefs being the very air which the broadcaster breathes, these have become issues of contention and debate (p. 627).

As a consequence, broadcasting's quest for explanations consistent with these faiths, what 'most people' used to think, has proved an increasingly difficult one, but not one on which it has turned its back.

Throughout the entire period this task has been pursued with vigour and diligence.

Illustrations: Man Alive, Nationwide *and* Tonight

The existence of the above preoccupations can be conveniently demonstrated with reference to a retrospective series of programmes called 'Ten Years of Man Alive', screened in summer 1976 between the end of *Man Alive* and the initiation of the *Man Alive Report*. This programme also reveals some of the ideological building bricks used extensively in the News and Current Affairs field to construct the public or national interest.

The principal aim of *Man Alive* was – according to Desmond Wilcox who was appointed co-editor of the programme with Bill Norton within the first few months of its existence – to focus on the problems and opinions of 'ordinary people'. In the retrospective Wilcox recalled that,

> many things have changed about *Man Alive* during those ten years but one thing always stayed the same. We've always believed that our programmes are first and foremost about people, *people like you and me, ordinary people.* . . . But, in fact, we've always confirmed – when we went out and listened to them – that there's really no such thing as ordinary people (BBC 2, 2 August, 1975).

The kind of events and people featured by this programme were not as a rule those who had gained high visibility in News. Indeed, its working definition of the 'ordinary' person was constructed against the images of 'news-characters'. *Man Alive*'s characters were 'ordinary' in as much as they were drawn from neither the ranks of reliable and authoritative spokesmen, nor from deviant economic and political groups involved in headline stories about such 'crises' as strikes or 'the state of the economy'. It covered a field of activities and people which had fragmentary and low News visibility.

The people and situations selected were signified, however, as 'extra-ordinary' in a variety of ways. Often they would be introduced to the viewer as 'seemingly ordinary', people who, on closer inspection, turned out to have endearing, though more often amusing peculiarities. Their 'peculiarities' or 'idiosyncracies' might be ordinary enough, but the people selected were depicted as having them to an exceptional degree.

One of the extracts in the second edition of the retrospective was taken from a report about 'a campful of nudists' and it included several sequences on a family and its problem of 'full time devotion to their cause'. This family is presented to the viewer by means of commentary over actuality film sequences. The commentary says

> All year round, happiness for the Lacey family means the hard road home to a bungalow well back in the woods near St Albans.
>
> Every evening Ken Lacey picks up his son Nigel and daughter Claire and they all drive home from work together. They seem a very typical family except that home is a nudist camp. . . .
>
> For the Laceys at any rate, their idea of heaven is to come home from work, take their clothes off, before they've even had tea, and relax.

In a similar vein, there were two other items – one about phobias and another about 'animal lovers who were almost suffocatingly filled with affection for their pet'. The first of these did not deal with 'the more commonly known phobias', but with a man 'who had a phobia, an incredible, but quite genuine phobia about leaves'. The other item, explicitly introduced as proof that there were no such things as 'ordinary people', depicted a woman cuddling and caressing her 'gorgeous cat' called Putsy which sent 'purrsday' cards to the woman's relatives. Each of these characters was presented as having something in common with others, and therefore some basis in 'normality', in the world of ordinary people. The Laceys were a 'very typical' and 'happy' family who did things 'together'; what set them apart was not just their nudity, which they had in common with others, but their full-time devotion to it. The lady with the cat not only possessed what was presented as a characteristic English trait – Wilcox's concluding comment had been 'Difficult to know what to say, isn't it, except that it could only happen in this country' – but did so in a manner that was eccentric.

But, characters such as these were not the programme's leading players; they provided *Man Alive*'s version of comic relief from the plight of its principal characters, the sufferers or victims of the problems that had seriously disrupted the even tenor of their ordinary, everyday lives. Among this 'troupe' were those who had had 'cruel humiliations inflicted' on them because 'they had all chosen to marry someone of another colour, what we chose to call a mixed marriage'. There were those 'families in which the oldest daughter was looking after the younger children because the mother had died or left home'. The programme that dealt with this was called 'A Proper Little Mother to Them All'. There were those 'little boys . . . being prepared with great determination for the large adult life' in prep. schools, in a programme called 'Who'll be Mother'. And a report about 'teenage fans whose behaviour was even then (1967) alarming a great many parents and making quite a few headlines'. In different ways, then, each dealt with 'problems' of family life.

Like other reports on different categories of 'social problems', these family problems were presented by means of a combination of actuality film sequences, actuality ('vox-pop') interviews, and commentary-over, exclusively delivered by the television reporter. (This format was changed in 1968 to include live studio debates and discussion between the protagonists who had been 'taking part in' the preceding film report – a symptom of the intensifying controversies which raged around the topics that were this programme's natural choice.) The interviewees – the subjects of *Man Alive*'s case studies – only appeared in the film reports narrating their experiences in response to questions from the usually unseen interviewer. They were typically seen in close or very close shot. A hallmark of this programme was the opening close-up on an interviewee in mid-stream, narrating what appeared to the producers who had selected the extract to be the essence of their particular problem. The formal techniques used by the programme had been adopted because of the effects of immediacy and unstructuredness they gave. This was such that the impression was constructed that the subject-interviewees were 'telling it how it really is', rather than 'how it seemed to be'. In other words, these techniques obscured the *interpretive* work done in and for each edition by the subjects themselves in making sense of their own situations, and by the producers in making sense, in *placing and locating* for the viewer, of the subject-interviewees' accounts. As a result, the network of ideological premises or suppositions which underpinned the accounts and explanations were reproduced as obvious.

The interconnecting commentaries delivered by Wilcox in the retrospective provide extremely rich evidence of the nature of this framework of assumption which informed the reports and gauged the subject-interviewees' problems. To introduce the story 'A Proper Little Mother', he said that 'John Percival had found another young girl who filled us all with admiration . . .', thus setting up a preferred attitude to the girl's coping strategies described in the report. The 'admiration' sprang from the girl's 'success' at *coping* with the situation. The commentary of the report itself highlights that she 'achieved a standard of cleanliness and efficiency that seems to have provoked some resentment in the neighbourhood. Nevertheless, managing the home, and especially the money, presents the same problems for her as it does many an older woman'. Subsequent sequences consisted of interviews with her brothers and sisters to discover 'how well' she managed to look after them and how she compared with the dead mother. Here then is an 'extraordinary' character who is considered and presented as such for a number of more positive reasons. She does what older women do, as well as, and in some instances, better than they do. Wilcox tailed the extract thus:

> We spoke to Carol Radford the other day. Now, she's happily married. Her husband, she says, is a marvellous man. And also now, she has two children of her own. But she's still looking after two of her brothers, who are eighteen and fifteen, and her sister who is thirteen.
>   Quite a success story.

This counts as a 'success story' in as much as the girl has not only coped with an abnormal situation in the past, but has through her own efforts effected a return to the indisputably normal – a happy marriage, a marvellous husband, chidren of her own to look after, and, as a bonus, two brothers and sister as well. In short, the explicit admiration stems from the perception of Carol as a 'super-normal'.

Not all characters featured have taken part in 'success stories', and not all are made to appear heroic. Many of the stories presented were tragedies in which the characters – for a variety of *personal* reasons – could not, or would not, make the return trip to the ordinary, normal world of nuclear family life. The mother, in the following extract from the story about sons and daughters 'forced to' look after aged parents, indicates how such characters – the tragic heroes and villains – were presented.

Based on social work case methods, the interviews were typically open-ended, and the interviewer did not much more than prompt the subject-interviewee to confess as fully as possible. But, in the following exchange, a different pattern can be deciphered:

AH (*interviewer*)	(*to mother*) What would you have liked to see him do in his life?
Mother	Well, I like him as he is, being at home with me, only what I've got . . .
AH	(*interjecting*) Do you think it is an unmarried son's duty to stay with his mother?
Mother	Yes, I think so, I think – I wouldn't like him to be away from me.
AH	Do you ever wonder if maybe he's given anything up to stay with you?
Mother	No, I don't think so.
AH	Well, I wonder if perhaps he might have got married . . .
Mother	He might've done, but I'm glad he didn't (*chuckles*). That's selfish, isn't it?
AH	No. Y'see you're in a difficult situation because you're old Mrs F . . . and you need a lot of help and your son gives it to you. And all he's complaining about, really, is that he wants a bit more life of his own.
Son	Look, that's a direct question, Mother, why don't you give a direct answer. I mean why can't you see that I want a little more private life.

In the course of this exchange, the interviewer moves from a low-profile prompting role into one in which she is the advocate of the son's cause. By the end of the exchange, she has stopped putting questions and puts accusing statements instead. The mother is here presented as refusing to negotiate, to make more 'bearable' a 'difficult situation' which has arisen, so it would seem, because of her age. It is this casting which licenses the outright, though mild, rebuke. Through the course of the exchange sympathy is transferred to the son. After all, is it not obvious that the mother is stubborn and perversely possessive of her son? That she is possessive cannot be denied. What can, however, is the assumption that it is '*her* fault' or the fault of her age.

Like the preceding extract, this one absents from the account any questioning of those *familial relations and expectations* that have bound mother and son together in a mutually destructive relationship. They are beyond question in these reports precisely because they provide a *measure of normality*: in this story, the absence of marriage for the son is presented as a yardstick by which her loss can be measured.

The family is used everywhere in the News and Current Affairs field in its assessments of the significance of big or troublesome moments in 'the life of the nation'. Nowhere is this more the case than in *Nationwide* (BBC 1). To discover what a recent Budget would mean for 'us', for example, this programme considered it 'through the eyes of three families, and, generally speaking most people in Britain fall into one of the three broad categories represented by our families here' (29 March 1977). The notion expressed here that most people in Britain would be 'represented by' one of the three families included in the programme was returned to by Frank Bough a moment later. He said:

> Well, our three families cover almost everyone in the country: the fortunate 10% of managers and professionals who earn over £7,000 per year; the less fortunate bottom fifth of the population who are the low paid earning less than £2,250 a year; and, the vast majority, somewhere in the middle, earning around £3,500 a year. And, we're going to start with a family in this category. . .

The families are here being used as *points of identification* for the viewing audiences. The family differs from other points of identification – wage earners, consumers, the fortunate, the less fortunate – in that it is often used not to point to or highlight differences, but rather, to highlight similarities. It is assumed to be something that 'most of us' have, and live out, in common: it is, in short, regarded as a *basic* social category, which is one of the pillars of 'national unity'. Such usage not only pre-supposes the widespread existence of nuclear family relations and the standard values and assumptions about the 'naturalness' of these relations, it also reproduces them as normal by offering the nuclear family as a category with which 'we all' can unproblematically identify.

But, of course, such identifications are problematic and for precisely this reason the process of reproduction is not always accomplished without breaks and resistances. I want to conclude by discussing briefly an example where the identifications and definitions offered by broadcasters *and* their authoritative sources are refused, and by so doing to emphasize that it is possible to articulate oppositional definitions via this medium.

Distribution of access to defining topics on television is unequal. Not all 'representative' figures are permitted access in the same way. The following example concerns a breakdown in the expectations which attend the role of being a member of an 'invited studio audience' and comes from an edition of *Tonight* (BBC 1, 9 September 1976) whose subject was 'Alcoholism'. It presented a studio discussion or forum on the topic which had already been covered by means of an investigative film report with John Pitman, formerly of *Man Alive*. The discussion was carried out between three of the 'experts' who had appeared in the film, set apart from the main body of discussants in the studio who were introduced by Denis Tuohy (presenter-chairman) as 'an audience . . . that includes other specialists on the subject and some self-confessed alcoholics and some regular drinkers who don't believe the problem exists for them'.

Prior to the discussion, the 'main points' of the preceding film were reprised by Sue Lawley:

> The main point the film was making was that many people are drinking more than they used to, and that social drinkers can become alcoholics without realising what's happening to them.

Standing behind a bar in the studio, Lawley then proceded to demonstrate the critical amounts of beer, wine and spirits by which drinking would have to increase to enter 'the danger zone'. The next section of the reprise was made up of extracts from the film and was tailed by Lawley thus:

> A mixture of drinkers who've recognised that they have a problem and drinkers who don't concede that there is one.

This theme was to play an important part in the breakdown of the 'orderly' conduct of the programme. This set-up, by which the topic was thematized for the purposes of the discussion, is hinged around the question of *self recognition*. It is also thematized as a *personal* or *individual* problem by means of such statements as 'how much do you drink and how much does it matter'; 'you don't immediately become an alcoholic . . .'; and, 'you may escape . . . of course . . . depending upon what sort of person you are'.

When the topic is passed over to Tuohy, he opens the discussion by *nominating* one of the experts in the 'audience' ('Dr Richard Parry, you're a consultant psychiatrist in charge of an alcoholic unit in Edinburgh . . .') to amplify a criticism that has been made of the film. Following Parry's comments, Tuohy hands the topic back to one of the experts who had taken part in the film:

> Well, could I put that back to Dr Griffith Edwards? And certainly the implication of the film was that quantity of alcohol did have some bearing on the tendency to drift towards alcoholism.

Griffith reaffirmed this quantitative connection, and the dispute between 'expert opinion' having been aired it is closed off by the chair:

> Well, can I at this point move from experts to ordinary drinkers. We've got three people here who admit that they drink regularly, and they admit they drink a fair amount. I'd like first of all, could you tell me, starting with, eh, Colin, how much you drink?

Colin   Well, its a long story see, but I've spent my life playing sport. I've been paid to play sport in my life. And during that life time I've drunk heavily. I'm a normal person.
    And a point you made earlier on, whereby your viewpoints are not normally accepted. So, therefore, if I were in a position with letters after my name and I said 'all people who eat too much cheese are going to finish up with heart troubles', would I be here then, would I. The fact is I drink now – so, when do I become an alcoholic.

This answer is a qualified acceptance of the interrogative put by Tuohy acting as chairman. While Colin opens by detailing his drinking habits, he then proceeds to comment on the *terms of reference* and how they have been arrived at. He refuses the simple quantitative definitions by offering his own biography as proof of their inadequacy.

Colin – we only know him as such – continues to voice his refusal of the definitions of the topic and of himself as one not conscious or self-aware of his drink problem. The latter gather momentum as Colin begins to interrupt other speakers. The following exchange is the last vocal appearance by Colin:

Tuohy   Can we go back to the row behind you again, Terry wants to come in. Terry you want to come in on that. Terry, what's your reactions to this conversation about the differences between people at risk and people who are convinced that they are not, and could not be at risk.

Terry   Well, quite frankly, I'm rather delighted by the reactions of the gentlemen in front of me [*Colin and friends*] because if ever there was a case of 'methinks he doth protest too much', there they are making a perfect case for the dangers of alcoholism. They really are. . . .

Colin   We're talking about statistics not about people. I haven't done it for
et al.   fifteen years. I was at a holiday camp and I did every single night.

Tuohy   So, what does that prove?

Colin   I . . .

Tuohy   Can I let Terry finish the point he was trying to make . . .

Colin   I'm going, I'm going, I'm sorry, I'm going [*walks off set; cut to long shot and pan Colin's exit*].

Tuohy Why are you going, you've got a case to make, can't you go on making it?

Colin OK, I'll carry on then. Let's . . .

Tuohy Right, but I don't want you to talk. I don't want you to talk all the time in a discussion in which there are 20 people. You've had more than your fair share . . .

Colin He's different from us. He's an . . .

Tuohy He's an alcoholic with a story to tell to the audience who are watching and listening to you, who are concerned about the problem, who are interested in your point, who are certainly interested in his point, and I'm going to make sure that yours is not the only point that is heard. If you can't stay to allow other people to make a point, well then I'm sorry. But, I think that you are having your say, and I would like the discussion to continue. And, I would like you to continue.

Colin does not speak again, In the final summary of the main positions aired in the course of the discussion Tuohy excludes Colin by nominating another of 'the heavy drinkers', the one who has said least, to conclude.

The repressive mode of control applied in this particular exchange and legitimated by Tuohy's references to the audience ('who are watching and listening . . . interested in his point') stems essentially from Colin's refusals of the main definitions and of his own status in the exchange. He refuses the role in which he has been cast – 'a heavy drinker with a problem, even though he doesn't recognise it' – and attempts to become a definer of the problem. From an earlier counter-attack in which Colin argued that

> . . . you're saying you know better than the ordinary person. Everyone has got their own built-in system. They know how far to go whether they're doing anything. . . .

it can be seen that in terms of the self-recognition thematization of the topic, Colin occupies a position diametrically opposed to the one adopted and preferred through the combined actions of the chair and the experts who had participated in the original film. Against the position that people 'drift into alcoholism without realising it', Colin asserts that the 'ordinary person' is wholly self-conscious, knows precisely what is happening and when to stop. Both positions are within the same ideological framework – but at opposite extremes. It is this difference which culminates in the breakdown of the smooth passage of the preferred definitions and in Tuohy's disciplining of Colin. There are other reasons for this breakdown, such as the broadcasters' perception of studio forums as communicative situations in which it is difficult to maintain a balanced, representative and 'fair' exposition of the topic, and their estimation, on this occasion, that Colin was simply an aggressive drunk who had stepped out of line. It can certainly be argued that although Colin's interventions establish an alternative definition of the topic, they were hardly adequate, and it can also be argued that they were not as effective as they might have been given his lack of skill in making the rules of 'fair exchange' which govern such communicative situations work to his advantage (for an account of a 'successful' intervention, cf. Connell, *et al.*, 1976). Nevertheless, this example demonstrates the very real possibility of using such situations to advance alternative definitions.

Conclusions

The above examples demonstrate that television takes its material from the phenomenal level of social existence – the level, that is, on which fundamental structural relations are encountered, lived and spoken out. The coverage of this material is not, as a rule, 'biased'. The systematic preference for only one side of a dispute about serious matters is a coercive form of discourse that has not, yet, been considered an everyday necessity. But neither is the concept of absolute autonomy, of non-correspondence between what is said in television's discourse and the continued political and economic rule of a particular class faction, adequate. If this discourse does not reproduce and attempt to amplify only one interpretation of a given situation, neither does it reproduce any and every in exactly the same way. Only a certain set of interpretations, in which some particular interpretations may well be mutually antagonistic, are routinely accorded a preferred passage through television's discourse. This set includes only those interpretations with which, it is assumed, 'many of us', if not 'all of us' agree.

Television's work of *informed speculation* – 'serious discussion on the basis of reality' as Sir Charles Curran (1974, p. 782) has called it – seeks to construct and elaborate the 'national' significance of the issues brought to its attention. In questioning the definitions of those directly involved in disputes, the role adopted by broadcasters is that of representatives of the 'national interest'. This ideological effect, what we may think of as the 'nationalization-effect', is attempted in a variety of ways. We have seen that certain of the typifications employed by the discourse are not overtly discussed. What constitutes 'a very typical family', for example, is not a subject for discussion on television. Rather it is one of a body of unquestioned constructs; it is a typification the meaning of which broadcasters unhesitatingly assume to be already known and taken for granted. Indeed, the hegemonic power of this typification and others like it – 'most people', 'many of us', 'the-nation-as-a-whole' – would be diminished by any elaboration. Their potential power to membership, to win over those viewing to the preferred definitions, depends precisely on their vagueness.

This winning-over is also attempted through the various categories of participants. The manner in which a particular character is depicted in the discourse has consequences for the relations established between the character and the audience. Interviewees, for example, are only rarely depicted talking direct to camera. For most television programmes, it is usually only the media professionals in the communicative roles of presenters, announcers or news-readers that are permitted to deliver what are known as 'pieces-to-camera'. This is perhaps the strongest form of address available in television discourse, in the sense that it is the form which most approximates to 'face-to-face' exchanges. Talking direct to camera contributes to the creation of a sense that the viewer is being spoken to directly, and therefore to an identification with the speaker's position. Talking at an angle to the line of vision of the camera has the effect of minimizing this identification with the speaker, and with what is being said. The speaker, in the role of interviewee, is not shown talking *to* the viewers, but, often to someone outside the field of vision. Showing interviewees in this way, creates some distance between them and viewers. Rather than promoting the involvement of viewers *in* the communicative situation, this mode of depiction casts the viewers in the role of *onlookers*. A perspective on what is being said by these interviewees is only delivered in the linking commentaries and pieces-to-camera provided by the broadcasters.

Certain types of participant are, however, permitted to have access to those areas of television's discourse where it is possible to reply to the overall summaries on film and pieces-to-camera. These include studio discussions and debates in which the broadcasters are present principally as time-keepers and referees. Participants have the right to speak here because of their already accomplished status in the other 'national' institutions. Television does not, on its own initiative, seek out 'representative' individuals whom it transforms into national heroes, heroines or villains; rather it reproduces, for the purposes of its coverage of issues, the apparent representativeness of these participants.

The skewing of access to these representative figures is no well-kept secret. It is, in the broadcaters' ethos, precisely what a balanced coverage of controversial issues is all about. If you want to know what the real nature of a problem is, its extent, or how it might be solved, where else could you possibly turn except to those organic spokespersons of the nation who have been mandated to resolve the conflicts of civil society? The potential effect of doing so is to reproduce the notion that all such conflicts are reconcilable.

However, as with all types of *social reproduction*, perfect harmony cannot be assumed. Actual work, sometimes as difficult as that in which Tuohy had to engage in order to maintain some semblance of an 'orderly exchange of views', has to be done in every programme, in every moment of signification, if resolutions with which 'we can all agree' are to be realized. Though the antagonisms between participants in programmes may not be of a fundamental kind – class antagonisms, fought out as such – they remain real nonetheless. They do make available alternatives and create cracks in the image that there can be 'national' agreements upon issues.

Nor can it be assumed that all audiences will adopt, without qualification, the orientations and positions that have been constructed in the discourse. It is certainly the case that not all the typifications employed by broadcasters draw attention to themselves. They will often pass without notice, without arresting our attention and without raising questions as to their appropriateness. That they can do so is a consequence of the continuing efficacy of ruling ideas, of a shared agreement and reciprocity of perspectives between broadcasters and their audiences. Not all typifications operate in this way. It is not at all certain that the typifications of groups of strikers as 'militants' or 'extremists' will serve the intended purpose of isolating them from the 'rest of us'. The typifications employed by broadcasters are capable of sustaining more than one meaning, and certainly more than their intended meanings. The gaps and discontinuities in the exchange with audiences which can and do arise – in the first instance, through those openings in the regulated disputes presented in programmes – cannot simply be regarded as mere aberrancies that need to be minimized. The moment of exchange is the site of a real struggle over definitions which requires study and clarification, and political development.

In other words, the reproduction of the 'structure in dominance' always takes place on ground on which struggle – ultimately a struggle between the fundamental classes – is present. Since the attempted ideological reproduction of the existing political and economic order is always the result of the contradictory relations of class forces, some of the secondary contradictions we have mentioned cannot be reconciled or moderated out of existence. The ideological work of television remains 'leaky', not just because the apparatuses and the institutions in which this work is carried out are too large as a result of the tendency to monopolization, but because the system it reproduces is contradictory. This should not obscure the fact, however, that the ideological closures toward which television's discourses tend overall are ones which perform functions for the dominant class *as a whole*. While the mode of realization is contradictory, it is by seeking out and defining the *'national'* interest that an ideological unity and coherence is provided for the dominant class.

BIBLIOGRAPHY

Althusser, L. (1971), 'Ideology and Ideological State Apparatuses' in *Lenin and Philosophy and Other Essays* (London).

Cardiff, D., Dyer, G., Cram, D. (1975), 'The Broadcast Interview', Central London Polytechnic (unpublished).

Clarke, J., Hall, S., Jefferson, T., Roberts, B. (1976), 'Subcultures, Cultures and Class' in *WPCS*, 7/8, Centre for Contemporary Culture Studies (Birmingham).

Clarke, J., Connell, I., McDonough, R. (1977), 'Misrecognising Ideology: Ideology in Political Power and Social Classes' in *WPCS* 10, Centre for Contemporary Cultural Studies (Birmingham).

Connell, I., Curti, L., Hall, S. (1976), 'The Unity of Current Affairs Television' in *WPCS* 9, Centre for Contemporary Cultural Studies (Birmingham).

Curran, C. (1974), 'Broadcasting and Public Opinion' in the *Listener*, vol. 91.

Curran, J., Gurevitch, M., Woollacott, J. (eds.) (1977), *Mass Communication and Society* (London).

Cox, G. (1976), 'Impartiality is not Enough' in the *Listener*, 20 May.

Day, R. (1961), *Television: A Personal Report* (London).

Gramsci, A., (1971), *Selections from the Prison Notebooks* (London).

Greene, H. (1969), *Third Floor Front: A View of Broadcasting in the Sixties* (London).

Hall, S. (1977), 'Re-thinking the "Base-and-Superstructure Metaphor" in Bloomfield, J. (ed.), *Class, Hegemony and Party* (London).

Marx, K., (1938), *The German Ideology* (London).

Murdock, G., Golding, P. (1974), 'For a Political Economy of Mass Communications' in Miliband, R., and Saville, J. (eds), *The Socialist Register 1973* (London).

Murdock, G., Golding, P. (1977), 'Capitalism, Communication and Class Relations' in Curran *et al.* (eds), 1977 (London).

Poulantzas, N. (1975), *Classes in Contemporary Capitalism* (London).

Swallow, N. (1966), *Factual Television* (London).

TONY RICHARDSON

SCIENCE, IDEOLOGY AND COMMONSENSE
On Antonio Gramsci and Louis Althusser

Without a doubt Antonio Gramsci and Louis Athusser[1] are the two most controversial and in many senses, central figures within the ferment that characterizes Marxist theory and politics today. Thus Gramsci is variously claimed to be the originator of a truly novel system of Marxist thought which transcends both Stalinism and Leninism. He is the theorist of revolution in the West and one of the key figures necessary to understand 'Eurocommunism', whilst alternatively, he is the theorist of the superstructure and specifically culture, in which guise he is the mentor of a culturalist reformist Marxism.[2] For his part Althusser, it is claimed, is a dogmatist, a structuralist, or, a profound Marxist philosopher. Thus, to use the words of the late John Lewis 'the Althusser Case' indicates a dogmatism 'a medieval variety. The prognosis is grave, the patient cannot last long'.[3] Conversely, Althusser is characterized as the originator of an authentic and rigorous Marxist theory, proof against ideological deformation by both bourgeois philosophy and politics alike. Whatever the stance taken it is testimony to the seminal nature of his interventions in the debates both within the French Communist Part (PCF) and in Marxist theory generally. The impact of his theorizing upon significant figures like Nicos Poulantzas[4] is very obvious and recently, with the publication of his self-criticism, he continues to figure very much at the centre of serious Marxist debate.

Before turning to the substantive objective of this paper, it might help if I were to set out my main guiding principles. Whilst this is not the appropriate place to reflect on them at length, I regard them as axiomatic to Marxist theory.

In the first place is the assertion of the primacy of practice. This is not simply to hold to the immediate reduction of all theoretical endeavour to the level of political practice, but to emphasize primacy in the sense Lenin indicated.[5] In the course of analysing the conditions which had been conducive to the success of the Bolshevik Party in forming the dictatorship of the proletariat, Lenin had stated, 'their creation . . . is facilitated by a correct revolutionary theory, which in its turn, is not a dogma, but assumes final shape only in *close connection* with the practical activity of a truly mass and truly revolutionary movement' (emphasis added). Or as Dimitrov,[6] general secretary of the Communist International had bluntly stated at the Seventh Congress in 1935, 'Revolutionary Theory is the generalized, *summarized experience* of the revolutionary movement' (emphasis in original).

A direct corollary of this principle is to emphasize that the question of the precise relationship of Marxist theory to the revolutionary movement becomes a prime issue in the analysis of any such theorizing. The unique nature of the fusion between theory and the practice of the masses postulated by Marxism points inevitably towards the role of the instrument or means of that process – towards the revolutionary party. It follows that the question of the status of Marxist theory and the role and function of Marxist philosophy has to be related both to the practice of the party and the working-class movement as a whole.

In the works of Althusser the question of the relationship between theorizing or theoretical production, as he used to designate it, and the revolutionary movement, was very much tied up with the problem of theoreticism.[7] His own self-criticism eloquently defined this error thus:[8] '[the] primacy of theory over practice; one-sided insistence on theory; but more precisely speculative rationalism . . . [rationalism] by conceiving matters in terms of the contrast between truth and error (that is Ideology/Science) – Speculation [by working to] conceive of established truths and acknowledge errors with a general Theory of Science and Ideology and of the distinction between them.' The additional charge levelled at Althusser by some of his critics, notably that his works, especially *Reading Capital* were characterized by a structuralist tendency[9] could also, in some senses, be related to the class or materialist basis of his position. According to Althusser himself, the structuralist charge was both misplaced and also indicated 'a secondary deviation'.[10] The gist of the accusation, was he claimed, to confuse his own, that is, Marxist theoretical anti-humanism with that of certain of the structuralist theorists. On the basis that both shared a certain overlap in terminology, it was then inferred that Althusser had become a 'structuralist'. The essence of the charge, however, struck at the basic materialist characterization of his theory, by inverting the relation of reality and theory. In other words, it was theory which now created the real in the sense that it was argued that Althusser shared a common position with those structuralists who asserted that the structure created the real. In short, Althusser was being indicted as an idealist. As he himself said[11] this accusation '[tended] toward the ideal of the production of the real as an effect of a combinatory of elements'. Concomitantly it was asserted that it was now theoretically possible to both construct and predict, a priori, a general theory of modes of production, including that of the communist mode of production.

In both cases the primacy attached to theory and the role of theory had immediate consequences for the form of the relationship between theory and practice. The primacy of practice was denied, resulting in a de-emphasis upon class struggle, especially the political class struggle. The crucial question of the fusion of Marxist theory and the labour movement was reduced to a technical question. The key role of the party as the instrument forging such unity was characterized in mechanistic and elitist terms, philosophically or theoretically established 'truth' had merely to be applied to the situation in hand. The issue of the status of that theory was to be resolved at the level of a 'General Theory of Science and Ideology', that is, at the level of epistemology – which assumed the guise and role of the guarantor of truth. The general category of epistemology – constituted philosophically, and in a relationship of externality to historical materialism – became the foundation of historical materialism and, in so far as it was characterized as speculative activity, led to idealism penetrating to the very core of Marxism.[12] Althusser, both in response to his critics and also because of his own self-evaluation and criticism, has now considerably modified his position. However at this stage it would be useful to indicate the essential feature of his changed position, which is crucially concerned with the nature of the fusion between theory under the practice of the masses whilst asserting also the key role of the party and its practice.[13]

In contrast, it can be said that Gramsci's whole life's work represents his assertion of the primacy of practice – of politics. More recent work in English[14] has provided us with a timely re-affirmation of the centrality of the political dimension in his work and a denial that his views on politics can be superficially characterized by reference to whether he was pro- or anti-Lenin. Even at the cost of stating the obvious it should be recalled that not only had he been a leading militant in the struggles of the Turin vanguard of the Italian working class, but that he was one of the figures instrumental in the creation of the Italian Communist Party (PCI). He was to become, in succession, the party's representative in Moscow in the Comintern and its general secretary, before being arrested and imprisoned by the Fascists.

The problem facing anyone studying Gramsci is to identify and follow through the complexity of his thoughts and the concepts he developed as he tried to reflect adequately upon a political life of extraordinary richness and variety. At no point throughout his works is the eventual goal of socialism lost. Thus, his views on the party – the 'modern prince' which has to assume the role of the collective educator of the masses – or on the specific nature of bourgeois class rule and how it contained the masses, are all informed by the belief in socialism and of the necessity of a strategy adequate to achieve it.

While not denying the goal of socialism, the latter day appropriation of Gramsci by Althusser and Poulantzas[15] has been accompanied by the characterization of his work as essentially historicist. In part, this results from his continued stress upon the socio-political function of theory, ideology and the role of the party, but it also serves to justify the particular form of appropriation and reading that is effected. Accordingly, Althusser claims that Gramsci tends to collapse dialectical materialism into historical materialism.[16] Philosophy is history. Marxism thus becomes, it is asserted, a world view – an ideology reflecting the development of the imminent tendencies of history. As such it is in a line of succession to the preceding great organic ideologies – for example religions. The fundamental advance achieved by Marx in creating a truly scientific theory of social development was lost. Marxism itself became relativized into one among competing ideologies. In turn, by a further series of reductions playing upon the socio-political function it could be collapsed directly into politico-economic practice. Instead of being capable of analysing the specificity of practices, the equation of practice with change led to the submergence of particular practices – for example the political, the ideological and so on, into a generalized or egalitarian concept of practice. In so far as this generalized concept of practice as transformation reflected the imminent tendencies of history, Althusser claimed that Gramsci had in effect fallen back into an Hegelian con-ceptualization of the totality – that of an expressive totality.

In a similar way Althusser tends to characterize as historicist many of the leading theorists of the revolutionary era of the October revolution and of the early twenties. During those days, and certainly in part reaction against the fatalistic policies of the Second International and also to the revolutionary fervour of the day, there was a tendency towards a voluntaristic politics. Lenin himself[17] had been moved to criticize such a tendency which was thus very much part of the context within which Gramsci was schooled. However, it does appear from his substantive writings that he did not immediately or obviously slip into this kind of reductionism. In his concern with the concrete, that is the situation in Italy facing the PCI, Gramsci continually emphasized the necessity for a correct analysis and strategy which would enable the creation of a truly organic party of the masses. In this sense, the fusion of theory and practice could be realized in a form adequate to transform societies.

Gramsci

Gramsci and Althusser as Marxist militants are, each in their different ways, concerned with the key relation of theory to practice. For Gramsci the Communist Party had to be the essential instrument or means of effecting the fusion of theory and practice. The status of Marxist theory emerged from the analysis developed by the party, conceived of as the collective educator. Insofar as the party was truly the organic party of the working class, theory emerged from within and in response to the problems faced by the organized masses. In this sense to postulate a philosophical endeavour to guarantee the truth or otherwise of theory would indeed have been to fall into a speculative metaphysics. For his part, Althusser has moved on from the project of constituting the scientificity of Marxist theory by reference to 'the Theory of Theoretical Practice' to a position which points towards a resolution at the level of the practice of a 'truly mass and revolutionary party'.[18] In interpreting the works of both theorists, a one-sided insistence upon the philosophical project of constructing either general theories of science or ideology, or exclusive concentration at the level of epistemology, should be avoided. Whether or not this line of argument 'bends the stick' too far in the direction of conflating Marxist theory into political practice, in turn reducing political practice into an undifferentiated notion of practice, remains a danger. However, a concentration upon the particular way in which both Gramsci and Althusser attempted to theorize and resolve the question of the fusion of theory and practice, would avoid any de-emphasis upon the crucial political dimension of their works. In turn, location of both of them within the particular context in which they intervened becomes possible and both the generality and the specificity of their theorizing – the distinctions they drew between the 'organic movements' and the 'conjuncture'[19] – can be fully appreciated.

In the case of Gramsci, the very complexity of the international and national situation of which he was a product and into which he intervened, cannot be adequately captured in this paper. In very broad terms at the international level, the early years of the Comintern (at least until 1921, when Lenin formulated the policy of the United Front),[20] were dominated by the belief that the era of socialist revolutions had begun. The 'model' revolution was that of the October Revolution, that is, the insurrectionary path. The defeat of the German revolution under the notions of the 'revolutionary offensive'[21] led to a shift in the Comintern policy towards the strategy of the United Front. A direct implication of the shift in strategy was that the leaders of the international realized that the relative stabilization of capitalist rule in Western Europe had to be reflected by strategy and tactics appropriate to the changed situation. Indeed, Gramsci himself was to write later[22] 'in the present epoch, the war of movement took place politically from March 1917 to March 1921; this was followed by a war of position whose representative – both practical (for Italy) and ideological (for Europe) – is fascism'. Whether this indicated prescience on the part of Gramsci or was merely written with the benefit of hindsight, it remained the case that both he and other leading figures in the PCI certainly remained sceptical of the United Front strategy, at least for the conditions prevailing in Italy.

It is, of course, very much by reference to those particular conditions that it becomes possible to locate the 'Leftist' policy of the PCI in its early years. During the course of the First World War, Gramsci, and for that matter, most of the leading figures of the PCI had been involved in the struggles of the Italian Socialist Party (PSI). Gramsci himself had been a leading figure in Turin where he was to become associated with the famous internal committees. The defeat of the factory occupation in Turin in mid-1920, was, according to Gramsci, in no small part, due to the ineffectivity of the PSI which was riven by internal factional struggles. One result of the defeat was to embitter still further this internal struggle and, as is well known, the PCI emerged in January 1921, the result of a split within the PSI. The leading figure in the new Communist Party was the formidable Amadeo Bordiga – for long a 'left intransigent'[23] within the ranks of the PSI. Thus, it is accurate to report that, if there was any one characteristic that could be highlighted regarding the infant PCI it was its sectarianism. As far as Bordiga was concerned, revolutionary purity was all – whatever the consequences it held for the development of the links between the party and the masses. For Gramsci, however, two factors were crucial. On the one hand he had been very closely involved with the Turin working class, so that he had not only become one of them, but was one of their leaders; in this sense he certainly realized the importance of working amongst the masses and of the value and limitation of 'spontaneous' activity.[24] On the other hand, he realized sooner than most of his contemporaries the danger of the Fascist threat and the fact that it was developing a mass base, especially amongst the rural petty bourgeoisie.[25] The continuing advance of Fascism in Italy in the early 1920s led Gramsci to question the sectarianism of Bordiga and its consequential danger of isolating the party from the masses. In turn, this led him towards an increasing concern with the role of the party as being the necessary factor of organization, the key to preventing the continuing advance of reaction and the decline of the progressive forces. In more concrete terms it began to lead Gramsci to accept the strategy of the United Front, albeit somewhat belatedly in view of the relatively entrenched position achieved by the Fascists.

Gramsci's arrest in 1926 and subsequent imprisonment under a sentence of twenty years removed him from active participation in Italian politics. Whilst imprisoned, of course, he commenced the mammoth task that was to become the *Prison Notebooks*. The actual conditions of their production, the censorship, the limited sources of reference allowed to him, and the precarious state of his health, added a further dimension to the difficulty of interpretation. His isolation from the contemporary political scene added a further complicatory factor. Thus, it is a source of debate as to whether his acceptance of the United Front strategy represented a continuity with his nascent thoughts generated by the political struggles of the early 1920s or, as has been argued,[26] was in fact a reaction against, and indeed a rejection of, the Comintern's Third Period line of 1928. I would assert that there can be no neat categorization – it is hardly plausible to ignore the changing ideas and political line that he developed in the 1920s – though concerned as he was with practical action and organization Gramsci hardly had time to reflect upon or theorize these events. On the other hand, it is difficult to claim or envisage that he had no views on the Third Period line and that it had no effect upon his writings. The report by Athos Lisa[27] to the Excutive Committee of the party in 1933 upon his release from the same prison that held Gramsci, and where he had had some contact with him, of course, adds weight to the latter assertion. For his own part, however, Gramsci characterized his prison writings in the following terms:[28] 'I'm plagued by a notion . . . that one has to accomplish something "für ewig", . . . I'd like to set up a plan for the intense systematic study of some subject that would absorb and control my inner life.' To this extent, therefore, the *Prison Notebooks* are preparatory studies towards fulfilling this wider project. In particular they represent Gramsci's reflection upon and generalization from his vast practical and above all political activities. The fact that he was never allowed to complete this task renders the job of reading Gramsci yet more difficult. However, the essential starting point is a close acquaintance with the political context, both national and international, within which he was a significant actor.

It is now possible to outline schematically the corpus of the theoretical concepts bequeathed to us by Gramsci. The entire *raison d'être* of his analysis is to establish the potential for political action and intervention; the immediate objective of such intervention was to shift the balance of forces in the direction of the progressive forces, the longer term aim was the winning of socialism. The key mechanism was to be the party – but not the party in any sense separated from the masses – but instead the 'organic' instrument of the masses. The views Gramsci propounded therefore provided the basis for the development of a new concept of the party – appropriate to the conditions of an advanced capitalist state. The party as a collective educator thus was to serve as the 'crucible' for the development of the organic intellectuals of the working class, and the practice of such a party would provide the basis upon which to develop further Marxist theory.

The concept of hegemony is usually indelibly associated with Gramsci and seen as his key concept, but this is an over simplification. I would argue that there is a unity to his concepts, explicable by reference to their overall political purport. Thus, the key concepts become – hegemony and coercion, the state and civil society, the historical bloc, the theory of the intellectuals both traditional and organic, the party especially conceived of as the collective educator, and the duality of strategy encompassed by the war of manoeuvre and the war of position. In turn, and very simply, these variously represent the condensation of the substantive analysis that he carried out of the forms of bourgeois class rule, its key mechanisms and the instruments and means necessary to transform such class rule.

The particular configurations of the historical development of the Italian nation was complicated by the advent of Fascism. This fact – whereby the bourgeoisie continued to rule despite economic and political crisis, albeit by 'exceptional' means – destroyed whatever credibility the gradualist policies of the Second International may have possessed. Throughout Europe as a whole the situation had changed from the possibility of imminent revolution – the war of manoeuvre, to the consolidation of capitalist rule and thus to the war of position. Yet, the advent of Fascism in Italy demanded further analysis of the specificity of that situation. It was to this end that Gramsci studied Italian history – crucially the history of the Risorgimento and the failure of the Italian bourgeoisie to complete its historic mission of founding the Italian nation and the Italian state. It was, at least in part, a consequence of this failure, according to Gramsci, that Fascism was able to develop in Italy. However, the Risorgimento was also complemented by the Southern Question, in particular the class structure in the South and the role of the Southern intellectuals – whose leading representative was Croce.

The interconnections between the maintenance of an advanced capitalist economy in the north and contemporaneously a backward and feudalist dominated agrarian south became a central preoccupation in Gramsci's analysis of bourgeois rule in Italy. Nevertheless, Gramsci certainly held the view that analysis of the enemy's forces was not in itself a sufficient basis upon which to frame strategy. The progressive forces had similarly to be subjected to rigorous analysis and if any Italian political figure on the left had direct experience of the masses – ranging from his childhood and youth in Sardinia to his leading role in Turin – then it was Gramsci. His early writings tend to display a belief in the value of 'spontaneity' – in the exercise of will – especially in the period during and in the immediate aftermath of the First World War. Following the reverses and defeats of the working class in the early 1920s however, Gramsci, came to see the necessity for an analysis of the limitation of such action, and above all, for the need for organization and education in order to extend and qualitatively change such spontaneity. Whether it is variously claimed, to this end, Gramsci owed more to Croce than Marx is not the most important point. The central issue is that gradually, throughout the twenties and more so in the *Prison Notebooks*, Gramsci began to locate the party as the agency of change. In turn, the party was influenced by the understanding it possessed of bourgeois class rule and its own location as a working-class party existing within such rule. To this extent the concept of hegemony and coercion encapsulated both the bourgeoisie and the working-class forces, and represented a key mechanism whereby the independent initiatives of the working class could be contained and transformed into the predominating terms and form of bourgeois class rule. Ideology thus became one of the elements whereby bourgeois rule was maintained, but it was to be situated within the wider concept of hegemony. The concept encompasses both consent and coercion and cannot be reduced one-sidedly.[29] To make such a reduction would be to fall into a mechanistic separation.

In this respect it is illustrative to take what Gramsci said about questions relating to ideology, commonsense, philosophy and so on. These concepts have to be located in the conjuncture which produced them and if we recall the political import of this analysis a series of important changes are introduced in the way in which we understand them.

For example, ideology. Instead of constructing a general theory of ideology in opposition to something called science and dealing at length with questions such as the truth or falsity of ideology, the question of false consciousness and so on, we are directed instead to questions like the following. Given the 'durability' of bourgeois class rule and its apparent reliance on both consent and coercion, what role does ideology play in maintaining that rule? If, as Gramsci indicated,[30] the concept of the historic bloc encompasses the politico-economic bases of class rule, then the rule of ideology as the 'cement' of that bloc points crucially towards analysing ideology as a practico-social force. As Gramsci put it:[31] 'Ideology itself must be analysed historically (in marxist terms) as a superstructure . . . one must distinguish between historically organic ideologies, those that is, which are necessary to a given structure and ideologies that are arbitrary, rationalistic . . . etc.' To the extent that ideologies have material force it is misleading and a deviation from 'the philosophy of praxis' to dismiss ideology as epiphenomenal and false.[32] The discussion on ideology leads directly into the understanding that Gramsci has of philosophy.

Schematically his treatment of philosophy leads into and connects up with the question of hegemony, its forms and its elaboration, the position and consciousness of the masses – or subaltern classes – and finally the commitment to changing that position by the creation of an alternative hegemonic force. In short, it leads to politics and ultimately cannot be separated from political activity and its direction. Thus, for Gramsci, philosophy does not mean, or – to put it more accurately – his concern is not with philosophers' philosophy, i.e. rational-speculative and essentially passive activity, but with philosophy in the sense of a conception of the world. Given the distinction between 'organic ideologies' and 'arbitrary ones', the thrust of the analysis becomes to understand the role that these conceptions of the world play in maintaining hegemonic order. In the last resort the basic ideologies arise in and from the practices of social groups, including classes; but they are not and cannot simply be reduced to simple reflections of such practices. The active development and elaboration of ideology becomes primarily the task of the intellectuals conceived of as a social category – the traditional intellectuals, or as the products of a fundamental class – the organic intellectuals. The process of such elaboration – the rendering systematic and cohesive – becomes an essential task. The ultimate test of the 'truth' of an ideology is[33] 'mass adhesion or non-adhesion . . . is the real critical test of the rationality and historicity of modes of thinking . . .'. Philosophy, therefore, for Gramsci becomes[34] 'a conception of the world and [that] philosophical activity is not to be conceived solely as the "individual" elaboration of systematically coherent concepts, but also and above all as a *cultural battle* to transform the popular "mentality" and to diffuse the philosophical innovations which will demonstrate themselves to be "historically true to the extent that they become concrete, i.e. historically and socially universal'. It is precisely the stress upon coherence and system which distinguishes a philosophy in this sense from what Gramsci terms commonsense. In both cases, the object of inquiry is to establish how such systems, when generalized, aid or are part of the given hegemonic structure. Commonsense – the historically produced conception of the world of the masses – is characterized by its being uncritical, disjointed and non-coherent.[35] 'It contains stone-age elements and principles of a more advanced science.' It also contains 'intuition of a future philosophy which will be that of a human race united the world over'. That is Marxism, arising from and in the action of the masses, 'when the group is acting as an organic totality'.

Commonsense also embodies notions such as 'being philosophical about it' – which, in so far as it suggest rational thought in contra-distinction to instinctive and violent impulses, embodies the notion of 'good sense', i.e. an aspect which 'deserves to be made more unitary and coherent'. The obvious distinction between commonsense and philosophy is that the former cannot be rendered coherent or unified. This fragmentation reflects the subordinate or subaltern class position and yet this limited form of consciousness of the masses cannot be explained simplistically at the level of 'self-deception'. Instead, it indicates 'profounder contrasts of a social historical order'. (Flashes of the group's embryonic conception of the world) may indeed appear 'when the group is acting as an organic totality'. But, this same group has for reasons of *submission* and *intellectual* subordination adopted a conception which is not its own, but is borrowed from another social group – hence the reason why philosophy 'cannot be divorced from politics'.[36] Thus, the role of ideology in maintaining the 'ideological unity of the entire social bloc which that ideology serves to cement and unify'. The maintenance of bourgeois hegemony, therefore, serves to maintain its directive role as a class, having its basis in both the economic and ideological. The effect is the continued submission of the masses, both by virtue of their exclusion from economic ownership and by their 'partial incoherent commonsense conceptions of the world'. In another section of the Notebooks, Gramsci related the notion of commonsense philosophy, i.e. a limited consciousness, to the concept of the economic-corporate. Whilst this notion can designate the stage of historical development of the state, in so doing it also relates to the 'relation of forces' – in class society the relation of political forces. Thus the economic-corporate level, the most elementary level, designates[37] 'the degree of unity and solidity within various professional and occupational groupings', including a realization of the need to organize within the group. A second level is that of class consciousness, still purely in the economic field, with organisation aiming at winning reform, etc., but only within the 'existing fundamental structures'. The third moment – which is the political, is the realization 'that one's only economic corporate interests transcend the corporate limits of the purely economic class'. The key element here is that it is at the political level and with conscious knowledge of that fact, thus achieving a 'unison of economic and political aims but also intellectual and moral unity, posing all the questions around which the struggle rages, not on a corporate, but on a universal plain and thus creating the hegemony of a fundamental social group'.

The struggle to transform the commonsense attitudes of the masses, therefore, is directly related to the political struggle against the dominant hegemony of the bourgeoisie and is also a task whereby it is necessary to build the hegemony of the masses contemporaneously. However, this does not lead to the conclusion that for Gramsci the ideological struggle alone is sufficient – it is at the level of the superstructures – at the political, that the decisive struggle takes place, but it must be remembered that hegemony[38] 'is ethical, political, it must also be economic, must necessarily be based on the decisive function exercised by the leading group in the decisive nucleus of economic activity'.

Finally, of course, the means whereby such struggle is organized and directed is a key element in the battle. At this level the analysis of philosophy and hegemony links up with the role of the intellectuals. The necessity of understanding the role of both the traditional and the organic categories of intellectuals had long been a concern of Gramsci but he now extends his analysis and understanding by relating the development of the organic intellectuals to that of the party. Indeed, the party now becomes the collective intellectual and the site whereby the unity of theory and practice becomes 'even closer'.[39] One should stress the importance and significance which, in the modern world, political parties have in the elaboration and diffusion of conceptions of the world, because essentially what they do is to work out the ethics and the politics corresponding to the conception and act as if it were their 'historical laboratory' – the relation between theory and practice becomes even closer the more the conception is vitally and radically innovatory and opposed to old ways of thinking. For this reason one can say that the parties are the elaborators of new integral and totalitarian intelligentsias and the crucibles where the unification of theory and practice understood as a real historical process takes place.

Althusser

Turning now to Althusser, there is an explicit concern with the current conjuncture, both theoretical and political, in which his writings are situated as reaction and intervention. Thus, to use his own words,[40] 'everything I have written, at first alone, and later in collaboration with younger comrades and friends, revolves, despite the abstraction of our essays around these very concrete questions'. The first task then is to provide an outline of this context and the particular issues of concern.[41] Schematically, at the international level, there was the death of Stalin, the Twentieth Congress of the CPSU, its critique of the Stalin years as the 'cult of personality' and the split in the world communist movement. In broad terms these events reflected in the lives of the European Communist Parties, including the PCF, of which Althusser was a member[42] – by creating a broader political space within which the party could function. In particular the party had a greater political autonomy and a concomitant responsibility to reflect and act both on its previous history and current policies. As Althusser recorded, the effects upon communist intellectuals of the declaration of the Twentieth Congress was expressed in terms such as Liberation, Freedom, etc. The spontaneous reaction which followed[43] drew heavily upon the early writings of Marx, especially the *1844 Manuscripts*, in order to ground themselves theoretically.

Add to these developments the relative lack of[44] 'any real theoretical culture in the history of the French workers movement', and the line of the Twenty-Second Congress of the CPSU, of 'everything for Man', and it becomes possible to locate and understand the influence of humanism in the theoretical writings of that period. The theme of 'man' and 'alienation' became the central concern. The building of socialism thus expressed an ethical postulate whereby man's potentiality was to be achieved and his essence restored to himself as a result of the ending of alienation. Of course, the concern with man had not just been a theme developed by Marx. It had a far longer history in bourgeois political thought. The question therefore arose as to the form and the effects that the insertion of an essentially bourgeois ideological position had upon Marxist theory and practice. Such questions and happenings provide us with some ideas of the effects of the conjuncture as it then appeared to Althusser at least. Whilst his own account is largely pitched at the level of 'theory' it should be obvious that far more than 'theory' was at stake. The resurgence of interest in the themes outlined above was also part of the attempt by the PCF to analyse the current conjecture and to pose a strategy adequate to such times. Yet, as Althusser stated, the end of dogmatism found the PCF in a position where it assumed that[45] 'politically and philosophically it had the only firm ground in the world', but lacked any convincing means of demonstrating this thesis, and yet was facing a present and future that demanded such demonstration, albeit its ill-equipment, in terms of Marxist theoretical resources, to begin the task. Given the paucity of the theoretical and cultural reserves of the French Party, the intervention by Althusser via 'theory' or 'philosophy' represented his contribution to the political and theoretical armoury of the party.

The links between the apparently unconnected concerns of Althusser – i.e. the analysis of Stalinism and the combating of economism and the critique of humanisn – can now be indicated with greater clarity. In the first place, it was the form of reaction to the experience of those years that troubled Althusser. How were the tendencies developing to be related to the corpus of Marxist theory? At this point the inadequacy of Marxist theory made it an obvious need to develop the level of theory. In turn any attempt at developing Marxist theory demanded a 'settling of accounts' with the years of dogmatism. The necessity for an analysis of the history of the Workers' Movement in the first socialist country became obvious. Moreover, the analysis to be produced had to be a Marxist, not a bourgeois, analysis, one that transcended the terms of individual psychology and which did not merely interpret Soviet development in terms of a breach of legal ideology. Ultimately what was at stake was the status of Marxism itelf[46] which was being called upon to account for its own history and development. To remain silent merely gave the lie to the opponents of Marxism and opened the way to their particular explanations, the neutrality and purpose of which could, to say the least, be questioned.

Such is the context in which Althusser has to be seen. To meet the problems described above – viz. humanism and economism – Althusser was driven to attempt to theorize the demarcation between Marxism and ideology on the one hand, thus in turn requiring him to indicate the scientific and theoretical bases of Marxism, i.e. historical and dialectical materialism on the other. From these twin objectives developed the characteristic elements of his theory – the notion of theoretical practice, the epistemological break, the science/ideology distinction, etc. Thus the notion of the break became central in establishing the specificity of Marx's discovery of historical materialism. The category of science was constitutive of the theoretical basis of historical materialism and served further to analyse the emergence of Marx's thought and in so doing to indicate its specificity. The necessity was to maintain the duality, historical and dialectical materialism, and in so doing to avoid either a reduction of philosophy into science, thus a collapse carrying with it positivistic overtones and consequences, or, of science into philosophy with the ultimate danger of subjectivism and idealism.

If Althusser was correct, then the reading of Marx which demonstrated the notion of the break, i.e. the constitution of the scientificity of historical materialism, also at one and the same time created the conditions for the birth of a distinctive philosophy, dialectical materialism.[47] The role of dialectical materialism in short becomes that of reflecting upon the development of historical materialism and producing the concepts adequate to that task. In order to do this the concepts of the problematic and the epistemological break were introduced – both of which were, according to Althusser, present in a practical state in Marx's works. The demonstration of the position was to be by the symptomatic reading.

Having made the claim on behalf of dialectical materialism that it was to be a theory of the production of knowledge, i.e. pitched at the level of an epistemology, Althusser had to indicate the distance between it and epistemology in the traditional philosophical sense, as constitutive of knowledge in general; for obviously this would deny the specificity of Marxism at the most general and fundamental level. On the other hand, he was then faced with the problem of the relation between scientific knowledge, Marxism and non-scientific, i.e. bourgeois knowledge, and the relation between Marxist philosophy and historical materialism. In order to meet the first problem, and to reject the couple empiricism/idealism, he stressed the 'interiority' of knowledge via the concept of the problematic. Knowledge could not be said to be knowledge in general but knowledges, i.e. the particular sciences. Since knowledge in this sense could hardly resort to an object outside itself (outside knowledge), that is in epistemology, in order to validate itself, the criterion of validity became internal. The epistemological problem, therefore, became that of the mode of production of a given science and its unity, that is constituted in its emergence from an ideological prehistory. The emphasis upon production/transformation, also emphasized the centrality of practice in Marxist theory.

The question now became that of relating dialectical materialism as a Marxist theory of knowledge to the particular sciences of knowledges without resurrecting the category of knowledge in general. Althusser thus argued that if the essence of knowledges lay in production/transformation then dialectical materialism had the task of reflecting upon the particular modes of theoretical practice – in so doing it would contribute to the constitution of a theory of theoretical practice *in general*. This is exactly how Althusser described and analysed Marxist philosophy.[48] The concentration upon a reading at the level of philosophy was to pose the question of the relation of philosophy to its object[49] and thus to indicate the specificity of its object and the specificity of its relation to its object. If the object of philosophy was a theory of theoretical practice in general, then the primacy of epistemology was asserted. On the other hand, there was a denial of an egalitarian concept of practice.[50] But it was difficult to avoid the point that theoretical practice was fully autonomous and constituted a hermetically sealed universe within which philosophical, i.e. speculative activity, was the order of the day. The emphasis claimed for practice either led to the assertion of an epistemology of practice in general, which was denied as a legitimate project, or dissolved practice into the practice of the particular sciences, i.e. a positivist error. The essential failure was the failure to spell out the connections between dialectical materialism conceived of in this form and the specific practices, in particular to indicate the precise function of dialectical materialism. Of course, for a Marxist and a communist militant, the failure to relate to politics and political practice was a glaring omission. As Althusser himself was to put the case later[51] he utterly failed to confront the crucial questions as to the unity of theory and practice and the fusion of theory and the Workers' Movement. The outcome was a 'unilateral' and 'ambiguous' definition of philosophy as the theory of theoretical practice, which he subsequently described as speculative rationalism.[52]

The question now facing Althusser was how to go forward, i.e. how to meet the objections levelled at his works by himself and his critics. It is to his credit that he did attempt the necessary reappraisal of his work, and that he maintained a committed stance.[53] The quickening tempo of political affairs – from May 1968 in France through Czechoslovakia, Chile, Portugal and Spain – but above all the development of the Union of the Left in France and the need to extend the role of PCF are all reasons why his analysis needed to be sharpened and extended. Moreover, the retheorized concept of philosophy both demanded such continuing reappraisal and was instrumental in it. In his more recent works, the concern with Stalin and with deviation – for example the economist/humanism couple – is linked to the overriding concern to produce a Marxist analysis of the Stalin years and the effects of that period. This is made against a background of the denial that the cult of personality/breach of socialist legality explanations constituted anything like an explanation. Such explanations are characterized as a right-wing critique.[54] Echoing his earlier strictures in *For Marx* he proposed the notion of an alternative left-wing critique and of the necessity of inquiring into the superstructure, the relations of production, class relations and the class struggle in the USSR.[55]

Given the leitmotif of the concern with the Stalin years, characterized essentially as economism/humanism and variously categorized as deviation or more recently error,[56] it is possible to illustrate the development of his views, particularly in relation to philosophy, via the 'stages' of development of these analyses.

Ironically the motivation in part at least to re-examine the role of philosophy was to be found in the precedent set by Stalin in his refusal to categorize language as part of the superstructure.[57] This indicated to Althusser the limits of class criterion and of the two sciences. Nevertheless, whilst his earlier texts had produced formulations of a number of central concepts, the failure to account for the predominant form of fusion between theory and practice at the political level led to the isolation of philosophy from political practice. This isolation was reflected in his reference to Stalin at that time, viz. whilst it was necessary to reject Stalin's system of government, it was possible to redeem him as a philosopher;[58] a philosopher that is, who – according to Althusser – both gave a lucid summary of Lenin's thought even though characterized by a certain 'pedogogical dryness' and who indicated the distance between the Marxist and the Hegelian dialectic. At a superficial glance, these statements may appear unexceptionable but, as Gerratana has recently indicated,[59] they reflect a more serious shortcoming attributable to Althusser's theoreticism and position on the autonomy of philosophy. They obscure a key question relating to

Stalin, namely the relation between Stalin and Lenin and the relations between theory and practice in Stalin. Of course, the need for a deeper analysis is obvious and the same need can also be found to be acknowledged in Althusser, especially in his retheorization of philosophy and with it the role of dialectical materialism, and the consequences for his theory of ideology and its relation to science.

Turning to this reformulation it is a comparatively straightforward task to describe its mechanics.[60] We find that by reading Lenin, especially *Materialism and Empirio-Criticism*, Althusser began to see the relevance of philosophy in such a way that it reflected class struggle and was not autonomous from it.

It is significant that it was to Lenin that he turned in order to 'found' his attempted reformulation because it both indicates the need to study Lenin apart from the presentation of his views by Stalin, and also points to the importance of the theoretical reflections of a man who was above all engaged in revolutionary practice and active as a leader of the first socialist state.

The provisional theses proposed by Althusser emphasized the practical social impact of ideology and the class positions represented in that domain by world outlooks, in the last instance, idealist (bourgeois) and materialist (proletarian). Similarly, in the domain of theory, according to Althusser, world outlooks are represented by philosophy. Philosophy represents the class struggle in theory. The immediate role of philosophy is to 'draw a dividing line' (Lenin), helping the people to distinguish between true ideas and false ideas. Hence philosophy is ultimately a political struggle. The reference to true and false ideas appeals not to a rationalist-speculative concept of truth but to the practico-social effect, in a way not far removed from one of the positions adopted by Gramsci[61] – 'in principle true ideas always serve the people, false ideas always serve the enemies of the people'. The initial role thus reserved for philosophy would seem to be that of critique[62] but the confinement of philosophy to that negative role alone does not represent Althusser's position adequately.[63]

So much for the 'internal arguments' of Althusser's changed position, the question is now to relate these to a 'quite different external logic'.[64] The clear characterization of the Stalin years as a deviation now emerges.[65] This is in opposition to the essentially one sided 'pseudo explanation', i.e. at the level of superstructure, the cult of personality. The effects of resorting to the essentially limited explanation of the 'cult' are, according to Althusser, to give a 'second wind' to both bourgeois anti-communist and Trotskyite anti-Stalinist explanations by providing them a space in which to insert their accounts at the level of the superstructure, opposing either Man to the violation of Rights or attributing the key role to the bureaucracy. Moreover, the effects in the west in the Communist Parties have been to emphasize humanism.[66] The bases and continuation of the practices of Stalin meanwhile continued, as did the presentation of the theory of Marx and of Lenin largely via the accepted orthodoxy of his formulations. The very absence of a coherent Marxist analysis of Stalin, however, creates problems for Althusser, thus he has a provisional problem of avoiding a pejorative dismissal *in toto* of Stalin. As he states, the consequences here would be to reduce Stalin to a *deviation* – the historical merits,[67] the construction of socialism in one country, the need to defend it against fascism, the necessity to build an industrial base, and the transmission of Marxist theory via Stalin would be prejudged.

With respect to his own analysis at the level of theory, Althusser has not adequately followed through the implications of his own position. Time and again, he has indicated that he is involved in a project to indicate the specificity of Marx's works[68] and to free Marxism from ideological or dogmatic readings. What applies to Marx also applies to Lenin, yet to state that one of the historical merits of Stalin consisted in the fact that he taught millions of communists, even in 'dogmatic form' that there existed principles of Leninism merely states the problem, which is, of course, that if philosophy is ultimately political intervention and reflects political and economic struggles then the relations between Lenin and Stalin becomes crucial. At the level of theory the hesitation by Althusser to draw the conclusions of his own position, merely serves to foster charges of ambiguity or, worse, that he is a recalcitrant Stalinist.

However, his most recent statement is far less equivocal.[69] The concept of deviation is replaced by that of error, the failure to provide a Marxist explanation is linked to the political and economic conditions prevailing in the USSR. Specifically in relation to philosophy, Althusser indicates how in the form presented by Stalin it had a practico-social function – not of critique but of justifying existing political practices, i.e. it was an internal ideology. Ironically, Althusser describes its practitioners as 'being transformed into headmasters of the school of theoretical production', among the effects of which is the unification and subjugation of the intellectuals.[70] (In a different context, Gramsci had also indicated how conceptions of the world ruling class ideology had served to incorporate the intellectuals and of the importance of this factor in the maintenance of hegemony.)[71]

The main value of Althusser's later position is that, by posing philosophy as class struggle in theory determined ultimately by politics, he has been able to move from a position of extolling Stalin as a philosopher to the realization that the forms of dialectical and historical materialism developed under Stalin are not 'innocent' and that dogmatism has to be located in a political, economic and cultural context and analysed in that context. As Grahame Lock has argued, there is the basis of real, left-wing analysis of Stalin in Althusser's work.[72] The plea for analysis and its political necessity have been stated by him: the problem remains of providing it and of thus avoiding 'the endless history'.

Conclusion

The relevance of studying Gramsci and Althusser is to establish linkages between them via the pressing and continuing political needs facing the Communist Parties of Western Europe today. On the one hand, the unprecedented opportunities open to them, on the other hand, the clear dangers that confront them. The charge of reformism, the pejorative use of the word 'Eurocommunism' by both the bourgeoisie and sections of the left, merely serve, in the absence of a clear analysis of our history, to confuse and demoralize. Above all there is a political need to 'settle accounts' with our history because to do so would situate Western communist parties in relation to the first socialist state and its particular history, and would enable those Western parties to theorize their particular practice and experience of the Labour Movement in the specific national conditions facing them. The obvious need for a theory of the superstructure, especially of ideology and politics, in order to achieve such ends means not only that we must examine the specificity of Marx and Lenin, but also that of Gramsci, and of Stalin too. Thus, whether there is a basis of a theory of politics and of the superstructure in Gramsci, for example, or whether there is a basis of a theory of the history of the USSR in Althusser is not only an academic problem but a political problem of the first magnitude. Ultimately, however, as even Althusser[73] has admitted, the final form of that theory will be found in the practices of the revolutionary party as the 'organic party' of the masses.

NOTES

1. A. Gramsci, *Selections from the Prison Notebooks*, translated and edited Q. Hoare and G. Nowell Smith (1971); *Selections from Political Writings 1910–1920*, translated and edited Q. Hoare (1977); Antonio Gramsci, *Extracts from Letters from Prison*, edited L. Lawner (1975). L. Althusser, *For Marx*, translated B. Brewster (1969); *Reading Capital* (with E. Balibar) translated B. Brewster (1970); *Lenin and Philosophy and Other Essays*, translated B. Brewster (1971); *Politics and History*, translated B. Brewster (1972); *Essays in Self-Criticism*, translated G. Lock (1976).
2. See for example P. Piccone, 'Gramsci's Marxism: Beyond Lenin and Togliatti', *Theory and Society III*, no. 4 (Winter 1976). For examples of the emphasis upon what I have termed essentially a culturalist appropriation of Gramsci see the various contributions appearing in *Telos*.
3. Althusser (1976), p. 53.
4. N. Poulantzas, *Political Power and Social Classes*, translated T. O'Hagan (1973); *Fascism and Dictatorship*, translated J. White (1974); *Classes in Contemporary Capitalism*, translated D. Fernbach (1975).
5. Lenin, 'Left Wing Communism', *Collected Works*, vol. 31, pp. 24–5.
6. Dimitrov, *The United Front* (1938), p. 125.
7. Althusser (1976), p. 1.
8. Althusser (1970), especially the English translation of the foreword to the Italian edition (1969), see also Althusser (1976), p. 102 et seq., and p. 124.
9. Glucksmann, 'A Ventriloquist Structuralism', *New Left Review* 72 (1972). See also Hindess and Hirst, *Pre-Capitalist Modes of Production* (1976), especially part 6.
10. Althusser (1976), p. 127.
11. Althusser, ibid., p. 129.
12. Althusser, ibid., p. 124, footnote 19. See also the definition of science offered at p. 112, footnote 8.
13. Althusser, ibid., p. 110 and footnote 5. See also pp. 115, 207, 208–15.
14. Anderson, 'The Antinomies of Antonio Gramsci', *New Left Review* 100 (1976); Mouffe and Sassoon, 'Gramsci in France and Italy – A Review of the Literature', *Economy and Society* 6, no. 1 (1977); Hall et al., 'Politics and Ideology: Gramsci', *Working Papers in Cultural Studies* 10 (1977); Davidson, *Antonio Gramsci: Towards an Intellectual Biography* (1977).
15. Hall et al., ibid.
16. Althusser (1970), pp. 134–5.
17. Lenin, op. cit. Note also that Althusser includes Lukács, Korsch and Luxemburg within what he designates as the leftist reaction to the Second International. See Althusser (1970), pp. 119–44, especially pp. 119–20 'Marxism is not a Historicism'.
18. Althusser (1976), 'Something New', pp. 208–15, especially pp. 214–15.

19. Gramsci (1971), p. 177.

20. See generally the reports of the Third Congress of the Communist International in Degras, *The Communist International*, vol. 1, pp. 306–16; see also *Outline History of the Communist International* (Moscow, 1971), especially ch. 2, pp. 95–158. Lenin's comments on the draft theses on tactics to be presented to the Congress included a sharp attack upon Radek for omitting to mention in the draft the 'importance of winning the majority of the working class', see *Collected Works*, vol. 42. pp. 319–20. Lenin also specifically defended the proposed tactics at the Congress, 'Speech in defence of the tactics of the Communist International July 1st', in *Collected Works*, vol. 32, pp. 468–77. Later he came back to the same theme, 'A letter to the German Communists', ibid., pp. 512–23.

21. Lukács was a leading theorist of the tactics of the 'revolutionary offensive'. See *Political Writings 1919–29*, translated by Michael McColgan (1972), especially 'Spontaneity of the Masses, Activity of the Party', pp. 99–105, especially pp. 102–4.

22. Gramsci (1971), p. 120.

23. The expressions left intransigent, maximalist, etc., were common parlance within the PSI and designated various factional positions within the party.

24. Bordiga's attitude to the Party can be seen in the so called Rome Thesis proposed by him to the second Congress of the PCI held in Rome 20–24 March 1922. In the course of the theses, Bordiga stated 'the essential task of the Communist Party in the ideological and practical preparation of the proletariat for the revolutionary struggle for the dictatorship of the proletariat is pitiless criticism of the programme of the bourgeois left . . .', see further Davidson, op. cit., p. 178. They represented therefore very much an attack upon and rejection of the recently formulated United Front policy of the Communist International. Gramsci, despite his relatively isolated position does seem to have opposed the theses from their inception. See further, Cammett, *Antonio Gramsci and the Origins of Italian Communism* (1967), pp. 161–2.

25. Davidson (1977), pp. 190–7, especially p. 193.

26. Anderson, op. cit., p. 59, where he claims that Gramsci rejected the United Front policy in 1921–24. By the time Gramsci returned to the question in the *Prison Notebooks* in the 1930s, the third Period line was Comintern policy. To the extent that Gramsci argued against this line by insisting upon the United Front it was 'a conscious break with his political past'. For a different interpretation see Davidson, op. cit., and Cammett, op. cit.; both implicitly argue for a greater continuity within his work. I would argue that the issue cannot be simply categorized in terms of continuity or break. To the extent that Gramsci reflected upon his past political practice, the germ of his acceptance of the necessity for a wider strategy was already present in this practice. See also the Lyons Theses (Cammett, op. cit., pp. 170–80).

27. On the details of the Athos Lisa report see Giuseppe Fiori's *Antonio Gramsci, Life of a Revolutionary* (1970), pp. 253–8.

28. Gramsci (1975), pp. 79–80.

29. See especially the arguments advanced by Anderson (1977), pp. 14–15.

30. Gramsci (1971), op. cit., p. 366 for the concept of the historic bloc.

31. Ibid., p. 376.

32. Ibid., pp. 164–5, especially 164, p. 377.

33. Ibid., p. 341, especially the relation of mass ideology to given historical conditions.
34. Ibid., p. 348.
35. Ibid., pp. 324–8.
36. Ibid., p. 327.
37. Ibid., pp. 180–2.
38. Ibid., p. 161.
39. Ibid., p. 335.
40. Althusser (1971), op. cit., pp. 15–16.
41. Althusser (1969), op. cit., especially 'To My English Readers' and 'Introduction Today'.
42. There is very little biographical information about Althusser in English. However, see the interview with Macciocchi, in Althusser (1971), p. 15.
43. Althusser (1969), p. 10.
44. Ibid., p. 23.
45. Ibid., p. 30.
46. Ibid., pp. 38–9.
47. Ibid., pp. 30–1 (see also Althusser (1971), op. cit., p. 19).
48. Ibid., p. 168.
49. Althusser (1970), pp. 14–15.
50. Ibid., pp. 58–9.
51. Althusser (1969), pp. 14–15.
52. Althusser (1976), p. 124, footnote 19.
53. Althusser, 'Lysenko: Unfinished History', *Marxism Today*, February 1977.
54. Althusser (1976), p. 82.
55. Ibid., p. 205.
56. Althusser, Lysenko, op. cit., see also Gerratana, 'Althusser and Stalinism', *New Left Review* 101–2 (1977).
57. Althusser (1969), p. 22, see also Stalin, *Marxism and the Problems of Linguistics*.
58. Althusser (1969), p. 97, footnote 16.
59. Gerratana, op. cit., pp. 102–3.
60. Althusser (1971), especially 'Philosophy as a Revolutionary Weapon'.
61. Ibid., p. 35 and footnote 35.
62. Althusser (1969), p. 29.
63. Althusser (1976), p. 146, *passim*.
64. Ibid., pp. 102–3.
65. Ibid., pp. 81–2.
66. Ibid., p. 83.
67. Ibid., pp. 90–1.
68. Ibid., p. 173.
69. Althusser, 'Lysenko', op. cit., see also Lecourt, *Proletarian Science?* (1977), Foreword by Althusser.
70. Ibid., p. 57.
71. Gramsci (1971), pp. 5ff.
72. Althusser (1976), especially the Introduction.
73. Ibid., p. 215.

GEORGE BRIDGES

WESTERN EUROPEAN COMMUNIST STRATEGY

The publication of *'Eurocommunism' and the State* by Santiago Carrillo,[1] leader of the Spanish Communist Party, has acted as a catalyst to discussion of the prospects for the left in the advanced capitalist countries in Western Europe. In this the strategies of the communist parties are a central point of interest.[2]

The background to this discussion includes the emergence of Greece, Spain and Portugal from fascism, the prospect of the left in government in France and Italy, the crisis of the international communist movement, and the digestion of the lessons of Chile. The post-war world has seen a stalemate in Western Europe. Does 'Eurocommunism' provide a feasible way out, or is it – as some have charged – incorporation of the left within social democracy.

The first problem is: what is the meaning of the term 'Eurocommunist', and how legitimate is it? The most vigorous opposition to 'Eurocommunism' as a term has come from the CPSU, mainly in the form of polemics against the leaders of the Spanish Communist Party, Santiago Carrillo and Manuel Azcarate.[3] However, what becomes clear when examining the *New Times* texts is the opposition not just to the connotations of the term 'Eurocommunism', but to *any term* which suggests a diversity of political tendencies, models of socialism and interpretations of Marxism. Such seems to be the significance of the assertion that '... there is only one communism'.[4]

This rejection suggests three negative possibilities. *First*, a blindness to reality: even a cursory glance around the world and the communist movement indicates that what is characteristic is diversity, especially in contrast to the past. *Second*, an attempt to divide communists and communist parties into 'real, honest, genuine' and those who 'serve imperialism':[5] this approach has a notorious history and can only worsen the atmosphere in the movement and obstruct the process of developing a constructive dialogue. *Third*, an attempt to reassert a new orthodoxy, expressing hegemonic ambitions of 'leading' parties: in this context the insistence in various parties, associated with 'Eurocommunism', on the primacy of the national determination of strategy,[6] as opposed to orthodoxy is itself an important break with the past.

It is thus explicable that Amendola should argue that 'there is no such thing as Eurocommunism' since 'there are as many specific strategies as there are communist parties'.[7] He is correctly emphasizing national diversity, itself paradoxically a vital element in the 'Eurocommunist' convergence. Togliatti suggested, in response to the developments after the Twentieth Congress in 1956 and the decline of Stalinist monolithism, a 'polycentric' system of relations. The reception for this, described by Boffa as 'diffident',[8] revealed, understandably, a widespread reluctance to revert to any form of new directing centre.

Furthermore 'Eurocommunism' is not itself an essentially regional or geopolitical concept. In the first place it is reflected in a group of parties not situated in geographical proximity (including the Japanese and Australian parties). In the second place, it goes far beyond the parties of the EEC in so far as it is a 'European' phenomenon. In this light it is better seen as a political tendency,[9] reflecting but not determined by geography, and stages of social, political and economic development. Looked at this way it has the potential to emerge as a trend, not only within the movements in capitalist Europe, but within the developed socialist countries as well. Thus, the trend represented by Dubcek, and the socialist opposition in Eastern Europe can be viewed in some sense as 'Eurocommunist'.[10]

It is of course true that the term did not find its origin in a conference of communist leaders, nor of Marxist scholars; but this in itself cannot invalidate its use. 'Eurocommunism' has established itself in the popular mind. It denotes an actual living reality ('we all really know what we are talking about'). Any attempt to 'liquidate' the term can only reflect a spirit of past heresy-hunting. This does not mean that Carrillo's reservations and caveats are invalid, but in Carrillo's words 'as long as we cannot find a better one',[11] we can do with what we have.

'Eurocommunism', in other words, has established itself as a political tendency within the international communist movement and its component national parties. It is not unified but represents 'broadly similar views'[12] partly corresponding to similarities in objective conditions, but also the outcome of definite political struggles. It occasionally appears as an informal grouping internationally, but is by no means a 'faction' with a common platform, nor a consistent intervention in the world movement. A range of bilateral meetings and statements have taken place over the last few years, but no general declaration. There is clearly an uneven development with a larger mass base in some parties and a longer historical implant in others.

The convergences of 'Eurocommunism' cover three broad areas, with a prospect of a fourth.

First, the problem of the nature of the transition to socialism in the social formations of advanced capitalist democracy.

Second, the nature of socialist society which emerges from this transition, especially at the political level.

Third, the nature of the world communist movement, and 'existing socialism'[13] embodying broadly shared responses to the lessons of the Stalin era, the invasion of Czechoslovakia, and continuing repression.

The fourth area refers to the European 'arena', in particular the emergence of supra-national institutions.

'Eurocommunism' has emerged as a confluence of four responses to history. The first is to structural changes in Western societies. Already the problem of whether the Bolshevik revolution could be emulated in Western Europe gave rise to controversy within the revolutionary movement, especially after the tide of revolution ebbed in the 1920s. Gramsci's seminal text on the structural differences between Tsarist Russia and Western Europe is fundamental to the thinking of Eurocommunists.[14] The ability of capitalism to survive economic depression, political crises and world war has rendered the frontal assault, 'war-of-manoeuvre', insurrectionary model inappropriate. The capitalist class has developed around it a strong network of alliances, a developed 'civil society' and a powerful system of mass consent (hegemony). An alternative approach based on the 'war of position' or the long haul is the characteristic strategic basis of 'Eurocommunism'.

The second is the assimilation of theoretical advances in Marxism, with the unlocking of Pandora's box made possible by 1956, signalling the beginning of the demise of the dogmatic Marxism of the Stalin era. The renewal of scientific socialism led to the 'discovery' (at least outside Italy) of Gramsci, the search for a Marxist humanism and a non-Stalinist interpretation of Lenin. 'Marxism–Leninism' and the rigid formulas which often accompanied it as a catechism, became increasingly demystified. Theoretical contributions from outside the

Marxist tradition, such as feminism, have been confronted to some extent, although as yet insufficiently assimilated.

However the attempt to legitimize 'Eurocommunism' as a 'new Leninism' seems illegitimate. Gerratana[15] has shown that the concept of Leninism itself is located within Stalinist ideology. This is not to question or dismiss any particular contribution made by Lenin, but to call in doubt in general the procedure of legitimation by reference to received authority. The elevation of Gramsci to Lenin's place on a pedestal will equally obstruct the need creatively to apply Marxism to current reality.

Furthermore the theoretical roots of 'Eurocommunism' are too diverse to be collapsed into a 'new Leninism'. It is true that Althusser has seen it this way,[16] but this ignores for instance the innovative contributions that he himself has made which have found expression in the model of the state favoured in Carrillo's book.[17] The Italian Communist Party (PCI) on the other hand not surprisingly draws heavily on the Gramscian heritage, though not uncritically. Carrillo is not afraid to conceive of his position as 'revolutionary revisionism'[18] which he claims is a definitive trait of all science. 'Eurocommunism' may well be open to the criticism that it is as yet under-theorized; there are pragmatic strands in the theoretical evolution, as Amendola acknowledges.[19] Carrillo, in giving credit to the work of the British party in elaborating a 'British Road to Socialism' in 1951, illustrates that the precursors of 'Eurocommunist' strategies located themselves in continuity with 'Marxism–Leninism'.[20]

'Eurocommunism' arises, in the third place, from a series of historical events. The failure of the revolution in the West in the 1920s, the disaster of Germany in the 1930s, the experience of the popular fronts following 1935, and anti-fascist unity in the Second World War were among the important developments leading to the abandonment of insurrectionist strategies.

The immediate post-war 'national roads'[21] and Communist participation in anti-fascist governments were an expression of the search for a new perspective. The impact of the Cold War in the late forties and early fifties implicitly raised the relationship between the CPSU and other communist parties, not just as a problem of the international situation, but as an aspect of national strategy. Monolithism was beginning to be perceived as a barrier to the emergence from isolation of the communist parties, becoming more overtly committed to democratic, pluralist strategies.

In this setting, 1956 signalled the critical break. The monolith began to crumble and the twenty odd years since have seen increasing tensions, including the 'explosions' in Eastern Europe, the Sino-Soviet dispute, the military intervention in Czechoslovakia and the increasing distance of key Western communist parties from the positions of the Soviet Union. The events of 1968 were catalytic, putting to the test many of the abstract formulas of international unity documents.

The strategic imperatives, as well as the direct analysis of the Czechoslovak situation, demanded a rejection of the Soviet theses and the actions which sprung from them. In general, the experience of the Prague Spring was evaluated positively, and was seen to accord with the strategic conceptions of Western communist parties. When *New Times* argued against Azcarate that he is 'unable to counterpose to the . . . experience of the USSR . . . any living practical embodiment of his own ideas',[22] the riposte could have been to point to the first eight months of 1968 in Czechoslovakia.

The fourth influence on 'Eurocommunist' strategy comes from the specific political situations facing the communist parties concerned. Internationally they are located between the two power blocs in an era of détente. The possibilities and dangers demand a foreign policy which cannot be reduced to solidarity with the Soviet Union. Autonomy in the sphere of international relations corresponds with a view of how to progress from 'bi-polarity' to 'multi-polarity'.[23] The emergence of European institutions (NATO, EEC) necessitates a regional convergence, but based on national autonomy. A limited 'national road' perspective needs to be enlarged to include a European dimension.[24]

The historical experience of democratic roads to socialism have been limited, but rich lessons are to be found in the Chilean events.[25] The avoidance of the fate of Popular Unity is one of the objectives forcing Western parties to deepen their strategic conceptions.

New possibilities have opened up the way for left or democratic governments in Western Europe, in particular the demise of fascist/military regimes and the challenge of the left in France and Italy. The ambiguities and tensions within previous party programmes have had to be examined and often revised. Emergence from anti-fascist militant illegality, or the 'ghetto' of sectarian politics, has demanded increased sensitivity to democratic structures.

Within the international communist movement events helped bring 'Eurocommunism' into a coherent form. The series of bilateral discussions around the 1976 Berlin Conference of European Communist parties helped counter the attempts by the USSR to win its positions. It led to a greater awareness of the common views of some Western parties. Internally the appearance of neo-Stalinist, 'pro-Soviet' factions and breakaways stimulated polemics which helped clarify differences.[26]

Before proceeding to discuss the areas of strategic convergence, it should also be emphasized that there are divergences. It is clear that within the societies of advanced capitalism there are important social, economic and political differences. The nature of class forces, the political protagonists, and recent histories, all contain very important distinctive features. Thus any attempt to transpose strategic conceptions such as 'historic compromise' or 'national reconciliation' to, for example Britain, would founder. Christian Democracy is not equivalent to the Conservative Party, which lacks both the popular institutional base and the social and political spectrum of the former.

We must also keep in mind not just the 'youthfulness' of the term 'Eurocommunism', but its varying degrees of acceptance even within parties commonly associated with it.[27]

'Eurocommunism' at the international level is really at the stage of being a proposal, an intention, a point of departure, not yet a point of arrival.

The first substantive area of convergence concerns the nature of the transition to socialism and the forces which will attain it.

This flows from an analysis of advanced capitalism which perceives the growing tendency to concentration and centralization of the economic sphere, and the growing role of the 'political' state in social life, as tending towards a basic polarity between the power bloc and the masses. This is expressed in the positing of a stage in the revolutionary process of a government, not yet socialist, but committed to advancing the interests of the people as against the monopolistic power bloc. This will be a government of a set of alliances, variously conceptualized as 'forces of labour and culture' (Spain) 'new historic bloc' (Italy) 'union of French people' (France) and 'broad democratic alliance' (Britain). It is undoubtedly a transcendence of the traditional formula 'working class and its allies', not just in the breadth of social forces referred to, but in the nature of their inter-relationship.

What is also being expressed is a view of capitalism which sees it as more than a mode of production which can be reduced to one central contradiction – between exploited workers and capitalists – and as a set of oppressions including those of race, sex and nationality.

This raises the problem not just of the breadth of social forces and of political alliances, but also of their 'depth'. It is for this reason that 'Eurocommunism' cannot be reduced to electoralism or parliamentarism. As Berlinguer makes clear in particular, an arithmetical majority is insufficient; what is needed is a political majority and a firm social base.[28] Within this new bloc there is complexity and even contradiction. Because of this the diversity and specificity of the components demand a pluralistic relationship. Without this the consent necessary for deep-seated social change cannot be generated.

The concept of the leading role of the working class has to be rethought in relation to the new strategy. In the first place the very definition of the working class becomes strategically significant.[29] The understanding of the relative autonomy of the political level of society and its centrality in a non-economistic revolutionary strategy means that the leading role of the working class cannot be reduced to its structural dimensions. As an historically evolved core it may be central, but this is always problematic.

The image of socialist consciousness developing from economic struggles plus propaganda also becomes inadequate. Winning a new hegemonic consciousness, one that seeks to transcend the forms of action which reproduce subaltern modes, demands that people experience in their daily lives not just visions of a new future but collective experiences that prefigure it. So a party, or labour movement, which seeks a hegemonic role within civil society must confront within its own ranks the oppressions, of race, sex or hierarchy, which form barriers to a new consciousness.

For the 'leading role of the party' this means a rupture with past traditions. The communist parties no longer aspire to a monopoly of power positions (not only in the process of taking power but in a new socialist system). Nor can they manipulate an alliance via a constellation of 'front' organizations. Nor can they act as if through the ordinance of 'historical inevitability' they had superior knowledge.

Nevertheless a democratic transition is not spontaneous; leadership and collective purposeful action are required. The leading role of the party is more as a generalizer, unifier, and strategist. It must aim to be hegemonic (in the sense of winning consent for its position) within the new historic bloc. Its leadership role is won through its ability successfully to pose realistic tasks which advance the revolutionary process. It has to reflect within its ranks the progressive elements of the new bloc.

What is clear, however, is that such a party is not the manifestation of an imaginary historical will but a synthesis of the elements it attracts to itself. Thus when Italian Communists argue that the PCI is not exclusively a Marxist party, it is not a revisionist heresy but an important statement about how its leadership as a mass party is to be exercised.[30]

The concept of the mass party refers, then, not just to a question of size, but to role, i.e. to the ability to act not as the vanguard of an insurrectionary assault, but as the organizer of popular consent to a democratic social transformation.

Gramsci's view that 'the revolution is not a thaumaturgical act. It is a dialectical process of historical development'[31] contrasts with the more traditional vision of 'come the great day'. The failure of this cataclysm to arrive, or the ability of the power bloc to forestall it, has entrapped the left in an historic stalemate. 'Eurocommunism' proposes the democratic strategy as the potential exit, succinctly expressed by Napolitano:

> . . . the only path that is realistically open to a socialist transformation in Italy and Western Europe — under peacetime conditions — lies through a struggle within the democratic process, a broadening of the alliances of the working class and its affirmation of hegemony and, finally, a gradual modification of economic and social structures within the framework of a still further development of democracy.[32]

This is the notion of the long, not smooth, haul, in which the limitations of 'bourgeois democracy' are burst asunder. It involves a challenge to bourgeois predominance by the new historic bloc in all spheres of civil society. It means enriching that society with new institutional forms of popular power and the creation of new political-social locations of hegemonic struggle.[33]

Far from being a capitulation to the social-democratic theory of the neutrality of the state, it is a perspective for a democratic transformation by which state power can be won. It is not a matter of avoiding the need to win from the ruling class the coercive power of the state, but of building a social-political-ideological base from which to do it.

Predominantly or ultimately militarist strategies of winning state power obstruct the achievement of a democratic base, and operate to confine the left to a permanent ghetto. In current conditions they either remain in the realm of rhetoric and sloganizing, or lead to urban guerrilla perspectives with disastrous consequences in Western Europe.

Nevertheless one of the interesting elements of the new thinking is a serious appraisal of the ways in which the political state can be confronted. The implications which flow from a 'smash the state' view are being rejected, and a more analytically developed approach adopted.[34] This involves the problem of the relationship between state and civil society, subordinating coercive institutions to parliamentary and democratic constraint, redefining their function, and reducing their scope, size and authority. It includes the intervention of popular hegemony within these institutions themselves, such as trade union and political rights, including the presence of the organized left. The experience of the Portuguese revolution showed the potential, in given situations for a popular, democratic role for the armed forces. Limited success has been achieved in organizing within the French and Italian police. An important part of Carrillo's book outlines a new military strategy for the left based on the notion of national popular defence.[35] Further winning popular hegemony within civil society will produce pressures which operate against acceptance of an anti-democratic hierarchy within the coercive institutions. Conversely the presence of an element of mass support for reactionary coercion, as in Chile in 1974, provides a social base for counter-revolution. The denial of political 'space' to reaction is thus the overriding strategic task.

A democratic transition will be a process involving stages, rather than a 'great leap'. This will mean defeats and retreats, sharp struggles and prolonged confrontations. Particularly complex will be the stage where a left or democratic government initiates structural reforms. In the conditions of general economic crisis there can be no millennial programme of rapid advance to 'socialism' or of dramatic advances in living standards. In this testing time, the maturity of the leading social forces in a broad alliance will be a determining factor in the ability to prevent a right-wing resurgence. Contradictions and crises can ensue, in which the critical factor will be the leadership qualities of the party and working class. Napolitano argues, with Gramsci,

> that the achievement of the working class's hegemony over other social
> groups presupposes taking into account the interests and tendencies of those

groups and reaching a 'certain equilibrium in compromise' with the working class not hesitating to make 'sacrifices of an economic-corporative character'.[36]

From this springs the deep need for the second substantive convergence of 'Eurocommunist' strategy – pluralism.

It is a strategy of pluralistic alliances and pluralistic struggle. The society which emerges from this process will take a pluralist form. Power and authority will be vested not in the revolutionary party but in the broad democratic alliance. The elements which comprise the alliance for change will not vanish or become subordinate to a 'universal caretaker' but remain to form crucial links in a system of power.

So the specific commitments of Western parties to multi-party systems of government in which parties freely contend for power, 'including those hostile to socialism',[37] are expressing a strategic imperative. It is not merely a matter of establishing 'democratic credentials' (important though that is). The defeat of political forces expressing capitalist power will arise as the outcome of political and ideological struggle. The enlargement and enrichment of the democratic terrain is itself a decisive weapon in a popular victory in this struggle, denying space to undemocratic and reactionary forces. This does not preclude the use of coercion, or legal measures against those challenging democratic, constitutional gains.

Part of this is the commitment to 'human rights', both those won, and needing defence, under capitalism, and those to be won in a new society.

A pluralist system does not only depend on institutional arrangements, but on the nature of the relationship between the elements making up the new historic bloc. Crucial here is the notion of autonomy, of the irreducibility of specific components to one 'central' element, be it the revolutionary vanguard, or the labour movement. Unless the autonomous existence within a broad alliance is projected to the structure of power under socialism, no stable alliance can be constructed. Specific social/political interests need space to pursue their particular concerns, because these actually reflect responses to oppressions experienced within capitalism – sexual, racial, national, etc.

These have a relative autonomy from the direct capitalist exploitation of the proletariat and at critical conjunctures can advance to the foreground of political struggle. Thus they cannot be seen as epiphenomenal or essentially reflective of one central oppression. While a socialized economy in a scientific sense may eliminate capitalist exploitation, there is no spontaneous automatic or overnight elimination of the *experienced* oppressions of capitalism. Socialization only provides the basis for this process, which is the outcome of struggle for prerequisite structural and ideological changes. This cannot be undertaken by a 'caretaker' party alone, however pure in intent. These battles need to be fought out pluralistically by a range of democratic movements.

For example, sexist oppression survives, and even tends to become institutionalized within a socialist society, unless there is a powerful and autonomous feminist movement. This must be free to battle against male-dominated structures and sexist ideologies even – and often especially – as they appear within the labour movement and revolutionary party.

While in principle this perspective is implicit in 'Eurocommunist' strategy, it is also true that a neglect of this particular question is a negative aspect of current programmatic work. Carrillo for example omits the feminist issue entirely.

More profound thought has been given to the question of trade union autonomy. By no means all the contradictions and antagonisms of wage labour magically disappear in a socialist economy. The 'rediscovery of alienation' in industrial situations in existing socialism points to the need for a genuinely independent trade union movement, with rank and file authority.[38] True, the social weight of trade unions nationally increases as they cooperate in determining national policy, economic planning and take on new responsibilities. Nevertheless they cannot be incorporated into the administrative machinery of the state, still less function as transmission belts for the Communist Party, without estranging the workers they represent at the workplace.

Establishing a strategic necessity for pluralism does not in itself resolve tensions and contradictions which can spring from objective conflicts, as well as ideological 'backwardness'. This need not be confined to the non-proletarian elements of a new alliance, since the transcendence of corporativeness is essential for working-class hegemony to be effective. Nevertheless it offers the most realistic way in which some of the repressive features associated with existing socialism can be avoided.[39] As such it represents a critique of, and a project to reform existing socialist societies.

This third element of convergence – the critique of existing socialism – has proved the most explosive aspect as far as other tendencies in the world movement are concerned. The *New Times*'s reaction to Carrillo's book went so far as to suggest that he was adopting 'crude anti-Sovietism' in the 'interests of imperialism'.[40]

The rejection of the old watchword, that the test of every real revolutionary was their attitude to the Soviet Union, is not just a moral reaction to the 1956–68 events but something which is necessitated strategically. No longer is the international dimension of nationally independent communist parties reducible to 'solidarity with the Soviet Union'. It is a recognition of the primacy, though not exclusivity, of the national element in revolutionary strategy. Nation states are the first political location of labour movements and popular alliance. As such a hegemonic strategy needs to pose national popular tasks.

In order to do this national autonomy of revolutionary parties is essential both for the formulation of foreign policy on a 'multi-polar' basis, and for the construction of internal alliances. Furthermore the thesis that socialism solves problems of the relationships between nations collapses in face of the evidence. The Vietnam–Cambodia conflict is only the latest in a series of problems between socialist states. This complex problem cannot be resolved by a choice of alternative 'leader' states or parties, nor posed in terms of accepting the hegemony of one of two power blocs.

The inappropriateness of the 1917 model of revolution in Western Europe extends to the political structures of existing socialism. Precisely how existing socialism should be theoretically appraised in the light of current Marxist approaches is an open question. Carrillo deserves credit for being the first Communist Party leader to raise this in a sharp way, although Togliatti preceded him in a more cautious questioning in 1956.[41] A whole range of structures – the caretaker party; the one-party power monopoly; the repression of criticism; the subaltern role of mass organizations; bureaucratism; and the scientific and artistic intolerance – associated with existing socialism cannot serve as a model for the democratically transformation of advanced capitalist societies.

The 'Eurocommunist' parties cannot be indifferent to events in socialist countries. The past compliance of the communist movement in Stalin's leadership helped consolidate his position and was thus co-responsible, even if indirectly, for the perversions of socialism. This compliance is not just a moral responsibility. Insofar as the perception of existing socialism as undemocratic by the masses is not a 'fraud' perpetrated by bourgeois media but corresponds to actual reality, it forms a barrier to democratic advance.

Furthermore this undemocratic model has not arisen in Eastern Europe spontaneously in accord with national circumstances, but has been 'exported'. Departures from the monolithic model, as the invasion of Czechoslovakia made clear, despite the formulas of international conferences, are not tolerated.

If 'Eurocommunist' parties are to receive the confidence of potential allies, they need to ensure that such a fate would not befall the implementation of a democratic transition to socialism. The best guarantee of this would be the democratization of existing socialism. Berlinguer rightly asserts:

> The workers' movement of West Europe is also called upon to give a possibly decisive contribution not only to the presence throughout the world of democracy and socialism, but also to the qualitative renewal in the sense of a full democratic development of existing socialist societies.[42]

This is not a goal exclusive to communists, although it is not shared by ruling circles in the West since such a project would help undermine their ideological influence on the masses. Participation in this project is most effectively made within the new tendency in the communist movement, a view largely shared by the socialist, democratic opposition in existing socialism.

'Eurocommunism' also represents an opportunity to find a new way out of the crisis of the international communist movement – a way which recognizes its diversity and proposes a model of 'unity in diversity' which is inclusive and consensual. It also foresees a developing unity not confined to the communist movement but of all progressive forces. Thus it involves an attempt to come to terms with the historical record of the communist movement, sifting out what was negative and sectarian. In the first place this refers to an historic rapprochement with social democracy, finally breaking with its characterization as 'social fascist'. As the difficulties in France of the Union of the Left indicate, this process is a complex and contradictory one. It cannot be reduced to a unilateral acceptance by communists of social democratic theses. But as Carrillo says, in light of 'Eurocommunist' strategies, 'there is no reason for not healing the split . . . and arriving at a convergence on the basis of scientific socialism and democracy'.[43]

This trend has also emerged with the trade union movement internationally, and within national movements especially in Italy. However, this is still a contradictory and tentative process and contrasting pressures have appeared, with an original and divisive social democratic trend emerging in Spain and Portugal, not to mention its continuing health in Britain and Germany.

The post-war Christian–Marxist dialogue was rich in revealing positive elements within some trends of Christianity, and this is partially expressed in the Italian 'historic compromise'. Reassessment of ultra-leftism, going beyond the past characterizations of Trotskyism as alien and conspiratorial, has been raised by Carrillo.[44] Ideological confrontation with mistaken strategies, rather than excommunications and manoeuvring, will not only be more fruitful than past approaches, but can also allow communist parties to learn from what is positive, questioning and healthily iconoclastic about new movements and ideas.

It is essential that there emerge a full historical analysis, based on objective research, of the Stalin era and its continuing effects within the communist movement. Recent works by Jean Elleinstein, and the discussion around John Gollan's article indicate that the ground has been laid.[45] Full cooperation by the Soviet authorities would facilitate this task, but lacking this, authoritative analyses from within the 'Eurocommunist' perspective are needed.

'Eurocommunism' exists, despite earlier reservations, largely within a specific geopolitical context. It is at one level an embryonic regional response to this reality. Institutions amounting to a new political, social and economic arena have been thrown up by post-war developments in the capitalist world. Some of these are inaccessible to the democratic forces, except via governmental participation, such as NATO. It is precisely the possibility of such participation as a result of left advance in Italy or France that is disturbing Western spokesmen like Zbigniew Brzezinski, David Owen and President Carter.

Other institutions such as the Strasbourg Assembly have elements of accessibility, and yet others like the European TUC are themselves products of democratic activity. While this is largely at the level of labour movement 'diplomacy', grass roots cooperation is developing.[46]

'Eurocommunist' parties have rejected a new regional directing centre. Nevertheless their strategy goes beyond the framework of 'national roads and in particular the Italian and Spanish Communist Parties have recognized the European dimension of a national popular perspective. The PCI has recognized European institutions as corresponding to objective trends in capitalist development, from which there can be no 'withdrawal'.

From this analysis comes a strategy for democratizing 'Europe':

> the immediate requirements . . . are the development of a mass movement at the European level, the creation of multiple centres of democratic control, and within the existing framework of the Community the struggle for the democratisation of the institutions of the EEC.'[47]

Most of the 'Eurocommunist' parties do not envisage a democratic left government withdrawing from NATO. The key task for a left government is to prevent reactionary forces from mobilizing their international resources against the democratic process. To block off this possibility means encouraging the détente process, reinforcing national independence while moving within the system of military blocs to a 'multi-polar' system. Thus foreign policy orientation would be neither 'anti-American nor anti-Soviet'. Carrillo sees an intermediate stage in the détente process between a bi-polar balance of forces and a disbandment of military alliances:

> We are not opposed to a phase in which defence is organized at a European level, independently of the United States and also of the USSR, on condition that such an organisation does not destroy the national character of the Spanish armed forces.[48]

This does not derive of course from a view of NATO as a benign, pacifist organization, but envisages continued participation in its structures as the best way to obstruct its use on behalf of reaction.

The appearance of 'Eurocommunism' in a militant and polemical form on the political arena has stimulated a wide debate. Most responses from the right conceive it as a dangerous Trojan Horse in which real intentions are disguised by hypocritical protestations about democracy. This is, however, to disregard the historic trajectory of the communist movement which cannot be reduced to a conspiracist interpretation.

From some quarters of the left, however, the main response has been to locate 'Eurocommunism' as a degeneration into reformism and social democracy.

Claudin's assessment, while repeating some leftist themes, has a more positive view of 'Eurocommunism's' potential.[49]

His first reservation is that 'Eurocommunism' has an overparliamentarist, over-electoralist emphasis. Revolutionary revisionism, or revolutionary reformism, certainly carries with it the danger of incorporation. However the concept of a hegemonic struggle goes beyond traditional debate about whether 'bourgeois democracy' can be transformed or smashed. It is not a question only of utilizing existing structures of civil society currently hegemonized by the bourgeoisie, but of creating new ones, and extending popular intervention into new areas. The dogmatic insistence of ultra-left groups on a 'soviet' model of power should not blind communist parties to the need for 'new forms of popular power' not confined to political institutions but extending to cultural, social and economic organisms as well. Thus it is not a question of challenging capitalism only on the terrain it determines, and playing the game by 'its' rules.

Claudin's second reservation concerns the rigour which 'Eurocommunist' parties bring to their relationship with existing socialism. Claudin bases his state capitalism/new ruling class model on the consubstantiality of socialism and democracy. This position however seems to preclude appreciating reality as too complex to compress into a Manichean schema. Bahro, on the other hand, attempts to analyse 'actually existing socialism as a social formation of its own type' and thus avoids *a priori* formulas.[50]

Claudin's analysis would logically lead to the exit from the world communist movement of 'Eurocommunist' parties. This would be tantamount to acknowledging defeat for the project of supporting democratic opposition tendencies. Further, it would amount to writing off any positive achievement of the past sixty years. This calls into question the very viability of the internal strategies. While Soviet triumphalism can be rejected, the existence of a bloc of countries in which imperialism has no sway is a crucial factor in the favourable world balance of forces. Without it countries like Cuba, Angola, Yugoslavia and Vietnam would remain within the orbit of imperialism. This does not lead to the conclusion that the Soviet Union is thereby a fully socialist society, but that a state capitalist analogy is inadequate.

Claudin's view is over-pessimistic about the potential for renewal and reform within existing socialism. The lesson of 1968 seems to indicate a trajectory of reform, rather than the revolutionary rupture logically consequent on Claudin's analysis.

This carries over to the revolutionary process in Western Europe. The absolutizing of a consubstantiality thesis leads Claudin to reject the notion of a stage of 'advanced democracy' where the left has governmental power, but has not yet made a socialist transformation. Claudin raises unrealistic expectations which cannot be fulfilled at this stage. Without the maturity of a hegemonic alliance, disillusion, despair and frustration can lead to adventurism, such as helped to isolate the working class in the Popular Unity period in Chile.[51]

Claudin's third reservation concerns the extent to which 'Eurocommunist' parties have drawn lessons regarding their internal structures and their relationship to the working class. His view that the continuing claim of some parties to be 'the' party of the working class is inconsistent with pluralism has some validity. So, in general, has his argument that over-centralism dominates the internal life of many parties. The demystifying of 'democratic centralism' is hopefully a future stage in enriching the new perspectives. However this is a complex question. In practice, whatever their broader ideological views, all parties which claim to be revolutionary operate a form of democratic centralism. Whether there is an alternative model consistent with the continuing need for effective leadership is open to question.[52] Nevertheless it is partly by confronting the criticisms of those like Claudin, who are prepared to look realistically at its potential and the necessity for new strategic thinking, that 'Eurocommunism' will develop greater sophistication.

'History' has the last word and as yet 'Eurocommunism' has to be put to this test as a strategy for transforming advanced capitalism and building a socialist, democratic alternative. Its success in some countries in mounting a viable challenge to the post-war domination of conservative and social democratic governments means that that test may not be long in arriving.

NOTES

1. *'Eurocommunismo' y Estado* (Barcelona, 1977); English translation, *'Eurocommunism' and the State* (London, 1977).
2. Among recent discussions available to an English-speaking readership are Carrillo (op. cit.); Eric Hobsbawm and Giorgio Napolitano, *The Italian Road to Socialism*, London, 1977; *Eurored*, 4 and 5; Louis Althusser, 'Revolutionary Strategy in France', *New Left Review* 104 (July–August 1977); Jäggi, Müller and Schmid, *Red Bologna* (London, 1977); Giorgio Amendola, 'The Italian Road – an Interview', *New Left Review* 106 (November–December 1977).

3. *New Times*, no. 26, 1977, p. 9, and the article by Uri Andreyev reproduced in *Soviet News*, 17 January 1978.

4. *New Times*, op. cit., p. 10.

5. Trotsky, Bukharin, Beria (though not Stalin), Tito, Nagy, and Dubcek are among the more famous Communist leaders who have been characterized as 'agents of imperialism'.

6. 'To be sure the line of development is towards the international, but the point of departure is "national" . . . it is in the concept of hegemony that those exigencies which are national in character are knotted together . . .' (Antonio Gramsci, *Selections from the Prison Notebooks*, London, 1971, pp. 240–1).

7. 'The Italian Road to Socialism', *New Left Review* 106, p. 50.

8. 'The Beginnings of Eurocommunism', Giuseppe Boffa in *Eurored*, no. 5, p. 6.

9. 'Eurocommunism: a reality, a hope', Azcarate in *Eurored*, no. 4, p. 5. Azcarate uses the phrase 'a new way of being a Communist'. And see Carrillo, op. cit., p. 8.

10. Stephen Cohen, in *Bukharin and the Bolshevik Revolution* (London, 1973), argues that some of the current themes in anti-Stalinism are pre-figured in Bukharin (see p. 384). The *Action Programme* of the Czechoslovak Communist Party in April 1968 could certainly be read as a 'Eurocommunist' document.

11. Carrillo, op. cit., p. 9.

12. The phrase used by Gordon McLennan, General Secretary of the CPGB, *Morning Star*, 4 July 1977.

13. With no brief to engage in the debate on the nature of socialist society, I use the term 'existing socialism', for much the same reasons as Rolf Bahro (see 'The Alternative in Eastern Europe', *New Left Review* 106, November–December 1977), p. 5.

14. 'In Russia the State was everything, civil society was primordial and gelatinous; in the West, there was a proper relation between State and civil society, and when the State trembled a sturdy structure of civil society was at once revealed' (Gramsci, op. cit., p. 238).

15. See 'What was the the origin of "Leninism"', Valentino Gerratana *New Left Review* 103 (May–June, 1977), p. 59 and reference in Hobsbawm and Napolitano, op. cit., p. 98.

16. Althusser argues that the Twenty-Second Congress of the French Communist Party 'simply adopted, in a new conjuncture, and with force, theses that Marx and Lenin had constantly defended (the peaceful transition is possible in principle, the broadest possible alliance is vital)' (*New Left Review* 103, July–August 1977, p. 15).

17. Carrillo makes this apparent in his chapters on the state, cf. op. cit., p. 27. It is in some ways unfortunate that Carrillo's book is being read as a definitive statement on 'Eurocommunism' since it has many weaknesses and ambiguities. These are partly explained by the conditions under which it was written, and its polemical nature.

18. Carrillo, op. cit., p. 17.

19. Amendola, op. cit., p. 44.

20. Carrillo, op. cit., p. 111. Even the iconoclast Carrillo uses an infelicitous phrase such as 'This is a Marxist truth' when referring to the state as 'the instrument of the ruling class' (p. 13).

21. Including, significantly, in Czechosolovakia.

22. *Soviet News*, op. cit., p. 23.
23. Carrillo, op. cit., p. 108.
24. '. . . Italy will not move toward socialism unless the European dimension of the strategy and concrete political initiatives of the PCI and PSI [Italian Socialist Party] are strongly developed . . . there has to be a common basis for seeking the road to advance to socialism in single countries of Western Europe' (Napolitano in Hobsbawm and Napolitano, op. cit., p. 77).
25. Enrico Berlinguer, 'Reflections on Chile', *Marxism Today*, February 1974.
26. Amongst these have been the breakaway in Sweden (see article in *Comment*, 6 September 1977), the Socialist Party of Australia, the Lister group in Spain and the formation of the 'New Communist Party' in Britain in 1977.
27. Cf. Gordon McLennan's statement to Thirty-Fifth Congress of the CPGB: 'We do not consider the term "Euro-Communism" is a useful or accurate one to describe this reality', reported in *Comment*, 26 November 1977.
28. Berlinguer, op. cit.
29. Cf. *British Road to Socialism (Draft)*, 1977, and Napolitano in Hobsbawm and Napolitano, op. cit.: 'I think that we must speak of the working class in a broader sense than in the past, that is, not only referring to manual laborers producing surplus value, but also to other strata of workers, whose objective placement in the productive process is very close to that of the working class and whose level of social and political consciousness makes an effective connection with the working class easier' (p. 55).
30. See Napolitano in Hobsbawm and Napolitano, op. cit., p. 94 and Berlinguer's reply to Bishop Betazzi in *Marxism Today*, January 1978, p. 18.
31. Gramsci, *Selections from Political Writings 1910–1920*, London, 1977, p. 92.
32. Hobsbawm and Napolitano, op. cit., p. 83.
33. See Althusser, op. cit.: 'They (the masses) will have to organise themselves autonomously, in original forms, in firms, urban districts and villages, around the questions of labour and living conditions, the questions of housing, education, health, transport, the environment, etc.' (p. 11); and Napolitano: 'a democracy exceeding the limits of traditional bourgeois democracy' (Hobsbawm and Napolitano, op. cit., p. 13).
34. See Jack Woddis, *Armies and Politics*, London, 1977 (particularly Chapter 13).
35. Carrillo, op. cit., p. 73.
36. Hobsbawm and Napolitano, op. cit., p. 73.
37. Cf. *British Road to Socialism (Draft)*.
38. See Mikhail Haraszti, *A Worker in a Worker's State* (Harmondsworth, 1977).
39. Claudin's views about the trajectory of Leninist strategies are interesting here (see 'Kautsky versus Lenin', *New Left Review* 106 (November–December 1977). Claudin's reduction of 'Eurocommunism' to a new Kautskyism, with hints of incipient Bernsteinism (p. 65) needs to be theoretically confronted. Carrillo's arguments (in Carrillo, op. cit., p. 151) are no more than suggestive.
40. *New Times*, op. cit., p. 11.
41. Carrillo, op. cit., p. 157.
42. Quoted in *The Times*, 3 February 1978.
43. Carrillo, op. cit., p. 104.
44. Carrillo, op. cit., p. 118.
45. Elleinstein, *The Stalin Phenomenon* (London, 1976), Gollan 'Some Problems of

Socialist Democracy', *Marxism Today*, January 1976, and discussion in later issues of that year. The publication of *Socialist Europe* by the British Communist Party's Soviet Studies Group has also helped.

46. For example the meeting of senior union officials in the car and aerospace industries of France and Britain, reported in *Morning Star*, 17 February 1978.
47. Don Sassoon, 'The Italian Communist Party's European Strategy', *Political Quarterly*, July–September, 1976, p. 275.
48. Carrillo, op. cit., p. 109.
49. Fernando Claudin, *Eurocommunismo y Socialismo*. This passage is based on a review by Peter Mason in *Eurored*, 5, p. 18, and a lecture given by Claudin in London, 23 October 1977.
50. Bahro, op. cit.
51. 'The real popular power was also weakened and the enemy moves facilitated by the acts of the ultra-leftists, who sought to turn the emergent organizations into a power alternative to the Allende government' (Luis Corvalan, 'The Unarmed Road of the Revolution', *World Marxist Review*, January 1978, p. 29).
52. Althusser discusses the problem, but although he notes that the 'new line' will have 'repercussions on the inner life of the party, on the forms of expression and freedom of Communists, hence on the *current* conception and practices of democratic centralism', he comes down against organized factions or tendencies (Althusser, op. cit., p. 18). In contrast it is worth re-looking at Roger Garaudy's notions of the 'cybernetic' model of party organization (Garaudy, *The Turning Point of Socialism*, London, 1969, p. 224). The British Communist Party was mandated by its Thirty-fifth Congress to set up a commission on inner-party democracy to report to the following congress.

THE CONTRIBUTORS

GEORGE BRIDGES was born in Dunfermline in 1941 and studied sociology at the Polytechnic of the South Bank. He is a lecturer in sociology at Woolwich College, and is on the editorial board of the journal *Eurored*. He was co-organizer and chairperson of the course on 'The Strategy for Revolution in Western Europe' at CUL 9.

IAN CONNELL was born in Glasgow in 1949 and studied English and sociology at Glasgow University. His article 'The Unity of Current Affairs' was published in *Working Papers in Cultural Studies*, no. 9, 1976, and his book on political television, *The Power to Define*, is scheduled to appear in 1978. He is at present a research assistant in the Primary Communications Research Centre at the University of Leicester.

SALLY HIBBIN was born in Tottenham (London) in 1953 and studied philosophy and physics at Keele University, where she was on the Union Executive. She is currently doing research in the history and philosophy of science at University College London. She was organizer of CUL 9.

BOB JESSOP was born in 1946 at Dartford (Kent) and studied sociology at Exeter University. He was a Research Fellow at Downing College, Cambridge. He is now teaching at the University of Essex and doing research there on state theory. His book *Traditionalism, Conservatism and British Political Culture* was published in 1974. He has published articles in *Sociological Review, The British Journal of Political Science* and *The Cambridge Journal of Economics*.

TONY RICHARDSON was born in 1943 in Hyde (Cheshire) and studied law at University College London where he subsequently did research in penology. He is a lecturer at Sheffield University where he is also doing research.

ANNE SHOWSTACK SASSOON was born in Santa Fe (New Mexico) in 1944 and graduated in political science at the University of California, Berkeley. She studied subsequently at the University of Padua, and at the London School of Economics. She is now a senior lecturer in politics at Kingston Polytechnic and is completing a study of Gramsci, the political party and his concept of politics.